THE TROPICAL AGRICULTURALIST

Series Editor
René Coste
Formerly President of the IRCC

Warm-water Crustaceans

J.C.V. Arrignon, J.V. Huner, P.J. Laurent, J.M. Griessinger, D. Lacroix, P. Gondouin and M. Autrand

Translated by Context Language Services
Translation edited by Dr M. Beveridge

Macmillan Education
Between Towns Road, Oxford OX4 3PP
A division of Macmillan Publishers Limited
Companies and representatives throughout the world

ISBN 0 333 57462 1

The Tropical Agriculturalist series originated under the title
Le Technicien d'Agriculture Tropicale published by G.P.
Maisonneuve et Larose, 15 rue Victor-Cousin, 75005 Paris,
France, in association with the Agency for Cultural and
Technical Co-operation based in Paris, France. Volumes in
the series in the French language are available from
Maisonneuve et Larose.

The opinions expressed in this document and the spellings of
proper names and territorial boundaries contained therein are
solely the responsibility of the author and in no way involve
the official position or the liability of the Technical Centre
for Agricultural and Rural Co-operation.

Published in co-operation with the Technical Centre for
Agriculture and Rural Co-operation, P O Box 380,
6700 AJ Wageningen, The Netherlands

www.macmillan-africa.com

Front cover illustration courtesy of NHPA / Daniel Heuclin

Printed and bound in Malaysia

2008 2007 2006 2005
10 9 8 7 6 5 4 3

Technical Centre for Agricultural and Rural Co-operation (ACP-EU)

The Technical Centre for Agricultural and Rural Co-operation (CTA) was established in 1983 under the Lomé Convention between the ACP (African, Caribbean and Pacific) Group of States and the European Union Member States.

CTA's tasks are to develop and provide services that improve access to information for agricultural and rural development, and to strengthen the capacity of ACP countries to produce, acquire, exchange and utilise information in these areas. CTA's programmes are organised around four principal themes: developing information management and partnership strategies needed for policy formulation and implementation; promoting contact and exchange of experience; providing ACP partners with information on demand; and strengthening their information and communication capacities.

CTA, Postbus 380, 6700 AJ Wageningen, The Netherlands.

Agency for Cultural and Technical Co-operation (ACCT)

The Agency for Cultural and Technical Co-operation, an intergovernmental organisation set up by the Treaty of Niamey in March 1970, is an association of countries linked by their common usage of the French language, for the purposes of co-operation in the fields of education, culture, science and technology and, more generally, in all matters which contribute to the development of its Member States and to bringing peoples closer together.

The Agency's activities in the fields of scientific and technical co-operation for development are directed primarily towards the preparation, dissemination and exchange of scientific and technical information, drawing up an inventory of and exploiting natural resources, and the socioeconomic advancement of young people and rural communities.

Member countries: Belgium, Benin, Burkina Faso, Burundi, Canada, Central African Republic, Chad, Comoros, Congo, Congo (Dem. Rep.), Côte d'Ivoire, Djibouti, Dominica, France, Gabon, Guinea, Haiti, Lebanon, Luxembourg, Mali, Mauritius, Monaco, Niger, Rwanda, Senegal, Seychelles, Togo, Tunisia, Vanuatu, Vietnam.

Associated states: Cameroon, Egypt, Guinea-Bissau, Laos, Mauritania, Morocco, St Lucia.

Participating governments: New Brunswick, Quebec.

Titles in _The Tropical Agriculturalist_ series

Contents

Foreword

Few tropical crustaceans are suitable for farming. Since the systematics of these species are better known than their ecology, only those species with a long tradition of natural exploitation, according to empirical rules based on observation of the animals' behaviour, have – in preference to other species – been the subject of zoological studies which might offer some hope of making their rearing more popular and more profitable.

This book deals with three shellfish. In section 1, the freshwater crayfish, *Procambarus clarkii*, is discussed in depth. The other two shellfish, one a chevrette or prawn (*Macrobrachium rosenbergii*) and the other a shrimp (*Penaeus monodon*), are marine or **euryhaline**. Their biology and rearing are examined in sections 2 and 3 in this book.

Section 1 deals with a single crayfish species, not for any lack of freshwater crustaceans – although admittedly there are more marine and lagoon species – but because only *Procambarus clarkii*, the Louisiana red swamp crayfish, seems to multiply without difficulty and even quite vigorously in subtropical and tropical waters. It therefore contrasts with the other known, popular species of which propagation in these same regions is limited by strict climatic and environmental requirements, along with disease hazards that currently rule out plans for their profitable introduction or farming.

This robustness has been observed in many tropical and subtropical countries, of which some are traditionally major consumers (Louisiana, USA) while others, such as Kenya where *Procambarus clarkii* was introduced only recently, now export it. This goes to show the species' usefulness, in the absence of other ways of exploiting wet areas with a view to increasing the value of **biomass** transformation.

However, despite the good qualities so promptly attributed to a new species, one must not overlook a number of disadvantages. These arise on the one hand, from the high reproductive potential of *Procambarus clarkii* which makes it a formidable competitor for other species of crayfish and, on the other hand, from a behavioural trait: in certain circumstances, the crayfish is a burrowing animal which can have harmful effects on the environment, especially in the hydro-agricultural field.

These disadvantages shed light on the understandably protectionist and restrictive attitude of temperate countries where other indigenous and foreign species are more suited to the existing **biotopes**. This is not the case in tropical and subtropical regions; here crayfish are non-existent and there is no lack of swamps. These, particularly in Africa, are unexploitable or unexploited as a source of human proteins, despite the urgency of the task. These areas could benefit from the introduction of Louisiana red crayfish.

Limiting the discussion in this book to only three genera of the farmed tropical crustaceans considered to be of worldwide economic importance is certainly an unwelcome narrowing of the field. Such a limitation can only be justified firstly, by the recent extension as a result of the acclimatisation of these crustaceans, throughout – and even beyond – the tropics, and secondly, because of the amount of work carried out on the methods and techniques employed which has encouraged this increase in crustacean farming.

The choice of three animals requiring different aquatic environments:
- *Procambarus clarkii*, which lives in fresh water
- *Macrobrachium rosenbergii*, the giant freshwater prawn or crayfish, which lives in both fresh and brackish water
- *Penaeus monodon*, the sea shrimp, which lives only in salt water,

involves a development policy which encourages a range of products with high marketable value, on aquatic sites which have been recently abandoned, e.g. salt marshes, or sites which up until now have had a low productivity, such as marshland.

Once there has been significant production over several years so that crustacean farming can emerge from the experimental stage, there must be a transfer of knowledge, techniques and husbandry practices to the operators in the field, farmers and potential farmers. This ensures that the technical and financial knowledge required is fully available and may well prevent failures as a result of ill-informed enthusiasm.

Jacques Arrignon

SECTION 1
Louisiana red swamp crayfish
(*Procambarus clarkii*)

1 The Louisiana red swamp crayfish – introduction

The Louisiana red swamp crayfish, *Procambarus clarkii* (Girard, 1852), is native to the central southern part of the United States of America. It has been introduced elsewhere, and is now found from the Atlantic to the Pacific coasts, throughout the whole of that part of the continent, south of the Great Lakes. It has been propagated worldwide, and expanding populations have been noted in the following regions:

Latin America:	Mexico (Sonora and Lower California), Costa Rica, Brazil, Ecuador
Caribbean:	Dominican Republic
Europe:	Spain, Portugal, France
Middle East:	Cyprus
Africa:	Kenya, Uganda, Zambia
Continental Asia:	Republic of China
Pacific Ocean:	Taiwan, Japan, Hawaii.

Aquarists and aquaculturists can now buy the species in places as different as Hong Kong, Singapore and Finland, so that by now it may have been introduced anywhere. For example, some individuals survived for many years in a small pond in southern Sweden but were unable to multiply. The emptying of an aquarium led to a large, thriving population in an urban pool just ten kilometres from Paris.

Procambarus clarkii accounts for roughly 85 per cent of the overall annual world crayfish harvest, with quantities in excess of 50 000 tonnes. Hence the importance of gathering the available information on the biology and rearing of this cosmopolitan species, which is both useful and harmful wherever its acclimatisation has been successful.

1

(c) Front view (photograph by J. Martin)

(a) Views of large *Procambarus clarkii*: mature female (right), immature male (centre) and mature male (left). Not ehter male gonopods and the differences in claw sizes (photograph by Jay Huner)

(b) Dorsal view (photograph by J. Arrignon) (d) exuviae (photograph by J. Arrignon)

Fig 1 *Procambarus clarkii*

Initial habitat

Introduction sites followed by acclimatisation

Fig 2 *World distribution of* Procambarus clarkii *(taken from Jay Huner and J. E. Barr, 1984)*

2 Biology

The biological information in this section may seem difficult to comprehend, despite the glossary at the end of the book. However, it must be understood by anyone wanting to develop crayfish production, whatever the species involved. Many of the commercial failures that hold back the rearing and exploitation of crayfish are caused by would-be producers who model crayfish farming on fish farming (pisciculture), usually because the two animal categories both live in the same environment, water. Some countries even classify crayfish under 'Fish' in their official regulations.

A crayfish has white blood, it has no bones, it walks, it can leave the water at night, it is equipped with powerful claws and can dig holes and galleries in the ground. All these characteristics and abilities, which are quite different from those of fish, must be explained to ensure that human intervention for rearing purposes is adapted to the specific nature of crayfish.

2.1 Classification

Procambarus clarkii is a crayfish, a crustacean adapted to a fresh water habitat. Crustaceans (of which there are approximately 26 000 species) form a tiny class of the vast group of Arthropods, jointed animals with a chitinous exoskeleton, which comprises about 1.1 million species.

Procambarus clarkii is one of the 400 known species of crayfish of the order of Decapods. This also includes the crab, the lobster and the majority of crustaceans which are of economic interest.

Two types of crayfish can be distinguished: those of the southern hemisphere belonging to the super family of Parastacoidea and those of the northern hemisphere, among which is *Procambarus clarkii*, belonging to the super family of Astacoidea. *Procambarus clarkii* belongs to the family of Cambaridae of which the natural distribution area lies in North America.

3

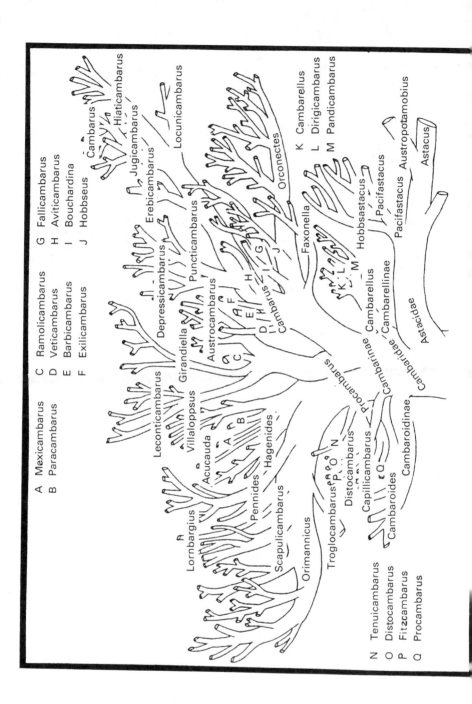

Fig 3 **Phylogenetic** tree of crayfish (taken from H. H. Hobbs Jr, 1972)

4

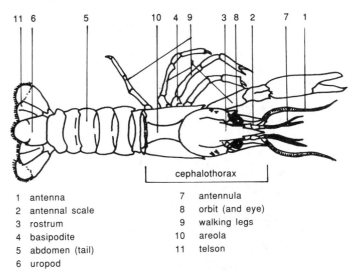

1	antenna	7	antennula
2	antennal scale	8	orbit (and eye)
3	rostrum	9	walking legs
4	basipodite	10	areola
5	abdomen (tail)	11	telson
6	uropod		

Fig 4 *Dorsal view of* Procambarus clarkii *(adapted from Jay Huner and J. E. Barr, 1984)*

2.2 Morphology

The body of the crayfish has three major sections: the head, the thorax and the abdomen (including the tail, edible for the most part). The head and thorax are joined and form what is called the cephalothorax. The body of the crayfish is divided into 19 segments, called somites, that are very visible in the caudal part, while 19 pairs of appendages, arranged functionally, are attached to the somites.

Appendages

The head carries the faceted eyes on eyestalks, together with five pairs of appendages:
- the antennulae
- the antennae ensuring the transmission and reception of sensory **stimuli**
- the mandibles
- the maxillulae
- the maxillae which tear and crush the foodstuff.

Eight pairs of appendages are fixed to the thorax:
- three pairs of maxillipeds (the third is the most developed)
- five pairs of walking legs (hence the name of reptant decapod).

5

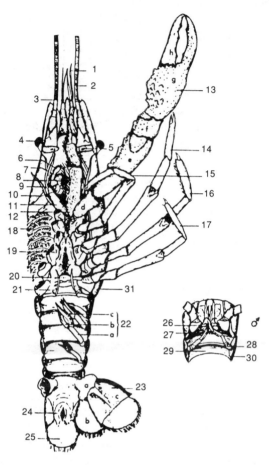

1 antennula	2 antenna
3 rostrum	4 eye
5 nephridiopore	6 first maxilla
7 mandibles	8 mouth
9 first maxilliped	10 second maxilla
11 second maxilliped	12 third maxilliped
13 chela (large claw)	14 first walking leg
15 second walking leg	16 third walking leg
17 fourth walking leg	18 gills
19 opening of the oviduct	20 seminal receptacle
21 first pleopod	22 fourth pleopod
23 uropod	24 anus
25 telson	26 genital opening (male)
27 first pleopod (male)	28 second pleopod (male)
29 sternum	30 tergum
31 pleuron	

Fig 5   *External anatomy (adapted from Jay Huner and J. E. Barr, 1984)*

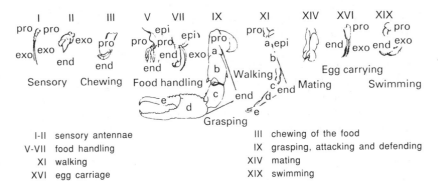

I	II	III	V	VII	IX	XI	XIV	XVI	XIX

Sensory   Chewing   Food handling   Walking   Mating   Swimming

Grasping   Egg carrying

I-II	sensory antennae	III	chewing of the food
V-VII	food handling	IX	grasping, attacking and defending
XI	walking	XIV	mating
XVI	egg carriage	XIX	swimming

Fig 6 *Appendages and functions (adapted from Jay Huner and J. E. Barr, 1984)*

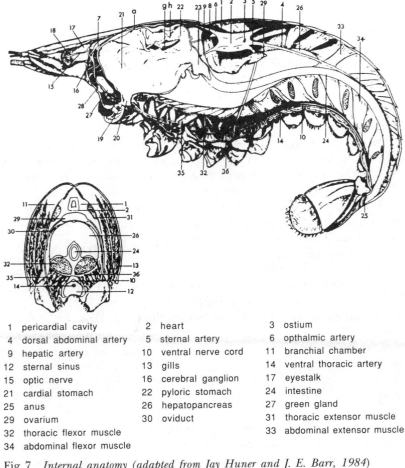

1	pericardial cavity	2	heart	3	ostium
4	dorsal abdominal artery	5	sternal artery	6	opthalmic artery
9	hepatic artery	10	ventral nerve cord	11	branchial chamber
12	sternal sinus	13	gills	14	ventral thoracic artery
15	optic nerve	16	cerebral ganglion	17	eyestalk
21	cardial stomach	22	pyloric stomach	24	intestine
25	anus	26	hepatopancreas	27	green gland
29	ovarium	30	oviduct	31	thoracic extensor muscle
32	thoracic flexor muscle			33	abdominal extensor muscle
34	abdominal flexor muscle				

Fig 7 *Internal anatomy (adapted from Jay Huner and J. E. Barr, 1984)*

The first pair of walking legs carries large claws, called chelae; they are used for food handling, fighting and protection. The four other pairs are used for walking and for cleaning the body; the last two have simple claws at the end.

The abdomen has five pairs of appendages and one pair of **uropods** which, with the terminal telson, form a sort of paddle which acts as retro-propulsive caudal swimming fan. These appendages play a reproductive role: in the sexually active male and during copulation, two pairs of legs are transformed into a sperm-carrying organ; the corresponding female appendages fix the eggs during their incubation.

Seen in cross-section, the cephalothorax is oval and the claws are more rectangular than round; these two characteristics are important for the animal's burrowing habits.

Exoskeleton

The crayfish has an outer shell, called the **exoskeleton,** consisting of calcium carbonate and a mixture of **chitin** and modified proteins.

The animal must change its shell during growth: moulting takes place several times until the animal is fully grown, after which it no longer moults.

Before moulting and as a result of hormonal changes, the shell loses some of the calcium carbonate stored by two small stones, the gastroliths, found in the organism on either side of the stomach. The loss of calcium carbonate causes the old shell to become friable and the crayfish can then get rid of it. The animal begins by slipping off its appendages then, with a flip of its tail, shakes itself free of the old shell, known as the exuvia.

After moulting, the crayfish absorbs water, grows and often doubles in weight. Its new shell remains soft for about 12 hours, then hardens gradually, thanks to the calcium carbonate in the gastroliths, the foodstuffs and the water itself.

The animal is capable of regenerating limbs or parts of lost limbs. Loss of claws is common in fights with predators or with other crayfish; the regeneration of appendages takes place at the expense of growth.

Colour

The chromatophore cells, located in the epidermis under the exoskeleton, are responsible for the characteristic colouration of every crayfish species. The Louisiana red swamp crayfish is mostly dark, blackish on the back and dark red on the sides when it is adult; young crayfish are predominantly brown-green. Colouring varies, depending on the environment and, periodically, on moulting which is preceded by progressive darkening. There are two recessive mutations: one pale blue, the other dark blue. There also exists a coloured form which, at maturation, is yellowish or orange on the sides. A pale white **phenotype** is also found, but it has normally pigmented eyes. None of these mutants has ever been found to represent more than 0.1 per cent of any wild or cultivated population or one which has returned to a wild state.

On being cooked, the crayfish turn red-orange.

2.3 Physiology

The structure of crayfish is very different from that of fish, which have internal skeletons.

Digestive system

The stomach, located in the cephalothorax behind the eyes, consists of two chambers of which the first contains three sorts of chitinous teeth that crush the food particles. After travelling through the second chamber and the middle intestine where the enzyme glands start the process of digestion and absorption, the food enters the hepatopancreas, the final and most important digestive organ of the crayfish. A rather short piece of intestine evacuates waste from the abdomen through the anus which emerges ventrally in the middle of the telson.

Circulatory system

From a simple, muscular heart set above the intestine and behind the stomach, arteries carry pale blood called haemolymph to the vital organs and the gills, where blood is refilled with oxygen and rids itself of carbonic gas and waste. Sinuses irrigate the different parts of the body. Crayfish have no veins and their circulatory system is said to be 'open'.

Nervous system

The brain of the crayfish consists of three nerve cell bundles, or ganglia, situated above the oesophagus. Two nerve cords innervate the ganglia of each of the body segments, stretching along the ventral side of the abdomen. The crayfish has a sophisticated sensory system, which is necessary for it to survive in an ever-changing environment.

Abundant sensory hairs, or setae, distributed all over the body, provide it with an acute sense of touch and balance, and its composite eyes ensure excellent vision.

Excretory system

The gills are situated on both sides of the cephalothorax, behind a sort of protective casing, inside a chamber which allows the water required for the gas exchanges to circulate. As long as the chamber is wet the crayfish can breathe, even if it is not in water.

The crayfish also excretes waste, in the form of ammonia, via the branchial chamber; the water flow expels the waste away from the animal's body.

The green glands, located on each side of the body above the mouth, act as kidneys and secrete urine which passes through the excretory tube into the bladder and then out of the body.

Muscular system

Powerful abdominal muscles allow fast retro-propulsive swimming. Other important muscles are lodged in the claws, legs, stomach and mandibles. The crayfish normally moves on its walking legs. Its usual means of locomotion is by walking. Swimming is only used as a means of escape. The animal lives on the bottom and along the banks of watercourses, rather than in fast-flowing regions of streams and rivers.

2.4 *Reproductive system*

The testicles in the male and the ovaries in the female are situated under the heart. The male has two **spermoducts** ending at the base of the fifth pair of walking legs attached to the thorax. The female has a pair of **oviducts** ending at the third pair of walking legs.

In sexually active *Procambarus clarkii*, male and female claws grow very considerably, as a result of maturity moulting.

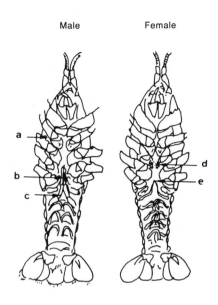

Male	Female		
		a	spur
		b	spermoduct opening
		c	copulatory appendages
		d	oviduct opening
		e	seminal receptacle

Fig 8 *Location of the male and female reproductive organs (adapted from Jay Huner and J. E. Barr, 1984)*

HOW TO DISTINGUISH MALE AND FEMALE

1 Look at the animals from underneath (ventral side).

2 Viewed from the head (cephalothorax), the female has no appendages on the first two abdominal segments, whereas the male has two large, horny pairs of appendages.

In the male, the two first pairs of abdominal appendages, the gonopods, become horny, and pronounced hooks appear at the base of the third and fourth pairs of walking legs. This dimorphism makes it possible to distinguish male and female immediately.

Before spawning, normally in a hole less than 1.5 m deep, the female cleans its abdominal appendages, or pleopods, with its walking legs. At the base of these appendages, appear pronounced glands producing a milky whitish, protein-rich substance. The female curves its abdomen in order to form a brood pouch and expels the sticky protein-rich substance. The eggs are also expelled, through the orifice at the base of the third pair of walking legs.

The fertilised eggs cling to the pleopods and are incubated in the brood pouch for between two weeks and several months, depending on the ambient temperature: at 20°C, incubation lasts approximately 20 days but below 10°C it generally ceases.

Biological cycle

After hatching, the **larvae** moult twice and are then able to leave their mother after about two weeks at 20°C. These young, now autonomous crayfish, can live for six to eight weeks without food at 22°C, and for much longer at low temperatures. The number of eggs depends on the size of the female. It is generally less than 50 for females up to 6 cm long and more than 600 for animals up to 11 cm long. It usually takes at least 11 months for the animal to reach sexual maturity, but this can be reached as early as 10 weeks at 22°C. Size at maturity, with overall length ranging between 5 and 12 cm, is subject to food, temperature, water quality, density and probably other, as yet unidentified, factors.

After the mating season, the surviving adults moult into the sexually inactive form (II), with its almost juvenile appearance. These animals then moult once or twice more before re-assuming their active form (I). Maximum life duration in the lowest latitudes does not exceed three years, but it can be as much as five years in higher latitudes.

2.5 Ecology

Robustness

> *Procambarus clarkii* is very robust and remarkably tolerant as regards water quality.

Generally speaking, the animal thrives best at the following values:

oxygen	> 3 parts per million (ppm)
total alkalinity and hardness	> 50 ppm (as $CaCO_3$)
pH	6.5 < pH < 8.5
salinity	< 15‰
	except for mating (5‰)

It can moult in distilled water and live more than three weeks without food or calcium in its environment.

As with all arthropods, its susceptibility to most insecticides is similar to that of the targeted organisms; however, it tolerates fungicides and herbicides when they are used in the doses recommended for crayfish ponds or adjacent fields where unwanted organisms have to be destroyed.

Since the gills are enclosed in a branchial chamber formed by side-extensions of the shell, the animal can take up atmospheric oxygen as long as the branchial chamber contains a little water. In a humid atmosphere, adults can survive out of water for at least three months. When the amount of oxygen in water falls below two or three **parts per million** (ppm), the crayfish makes its way to the surface and takes up atmospheric oxygen. Moreover, the animal is capable of living in entirely **anaerobic** conditions for 3 to 12 hours at a temperature of between 22 and 25°C.

Generally, the species tolerates extreme values in concentration in the water of salts such as nitrates, nitrites, ammonia, carbonic gas and hydrogen sulphide; it can withstand levels much higher than those at which tolerant fish are affected or killed.

Optimum growth is obtained between 22 and 25°C; temperatures above 33°C cause death within 12 to 24 hours, even for animals already acclimatised to warm waters.

Habitat

Procambarus clarkii is able to live in swamps alternately flooded and drained. This seasonal fluctuation encourages proliferous swamp vegetation on which the animal feeds during the floods. Draining eliminates predatory fish and invertebrates.

The largest concentrations of *Procambarus clarkii* are found in sunny stretches of water not more than 40 cm deep. The most favourable water bottoms are muddy and covered in semi-aquatic **lentic** vegetation rather than **lotic** plants.

Burrows

Procambarus clarkii is adapted to temporary drought conditions. When seasonal water variations occur, the crayfish digs a burrow as the flood recedes. It also digs a burrow whenever the water level drops, even in atypical conditions, regardless of the season: burrowing is vital to the **biological cycle** of *Procambarus clarkii.*

This burrowing behaviour – one of the animal's most remarkable characteristics – involves constructing a chimney around each of the habitat entrances. The crayfish begins by scraping the ground with its walking legs. Materials are propelled by the third pair of maxillipeds and compacted by the chelipeds into a sausage shape, which the animal moves, head first, towards the surface. Once there, the 'sausage' is tamped and shaped into a chimney by the claws. The crayfish goes back down tail first into the hole and repeats the process, which usually takes place at night.

Table 1 Plants recorded in Louisiana, USA, in the preferred habitat of *Procambarus clarkii* (adapted from Penn in Huner, 1984)

Level	Scientific name
Emerged plants	*Scirpus spp.* *Typha spp.* *Alternanthera philoxerides* *Ludwigia spp.* *Polygonum spp.* *Pontederia spp.* *Sagittaria spp.* *Eleocharis spp.* *Juncus spp.* *Bacopa spp.* *Hydrocotyle spp.*
Floating plants	*Eichornia crassipes* *Lemna spp.* *Azolla caroliniana*
Immersed plants	*Myriophyllum spp.* *Cabomba spp.* *Ceratophyllum spp.* *Najas spp.*
Plants withstanding periodic flooding	*Echinochloa spp.* *Panicum spp.* *Paspalum spp.* *Cyperus spp.* *Rhynchospora* *Carex spp.*

Table 2 Characteristic habitats of *Procambarus clarkii* in Louisiana (adapted from Penn in Huner, 1984)

Type of habitat	%
Swamps	35
Flooded forest	30
Ponds and burrows	14
Ditches	12
Canals and bayous	8
Limnocrene springs	1

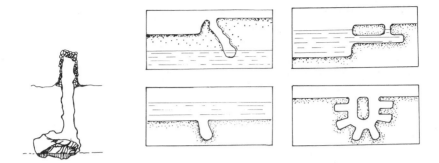

Fig 9   *Sections of a* Procambarus clarkii *burrow (adapted from Jay Huner and J.E. Barr, 1984, and A.P. Gaude, 1987)*

Fig 10   *Building a burrow (photo: J. Arrignon)*

Fig 11   *Habitat of* Procambarus clarkii *in Louisiana (photo: J. F. Martin)*

We can think of this chimney as a shaft improving the ventilation of the burrow, where water is generally low in oxygen. *Procambarus clarkii* builds different types of burrows. The simplest consists of a fully immersed hole, dug in the bottom of the pool or the watercourse; the hole is seldom more than 20 cm long and acts as a temporary refuge.

Burrows dug in the stream are more elaborate and make use of roots and waste material, as well as plant cover growing on the banks. The openings are topped by shafts and the underground gallery is divided into chambers about 20 cm wide. The depth of each bore is determined by the difference between the ground level and the water level. The length of the gallery is between 1.2 and 2.4 metres. A burrow is usually inhabited by an adult couple, the male defending the entrance, close to the surface.

Horizontal galleries, observed in California, Kenya and France, seem to correspond to stable water levels. Most are U-shaped and the branches form lateral chambers, lying on a horizontal plane. A vertical bore at the bottom of the 'U' leads to the open air.

In many cases, as a result of overpopulation or frequent changes in the water level, very sophisticated networks can be observed. These seriously damage paddy levees and dam dykes (Chapter 5).

ROBUSTNESS

Procambarus clarkii is not very demanding; it requires no particular facilities; it is mainly herbivorous and eats plant waste; it breeds quite easily, without human intervention.

Diet

Procambarus clarkii is omnivorous; it consumes a wide variety of organic materials, both plant and animal, along with waste. Most of the food is provided by aquatic and semi-aquatic plants found in swamps or alongside pools.

Animals form only a small part of the diet of the crayfish. Its amino-acid and essential fatty acids requirements (cholesterol, proteins, etc.) are met by the consumption of **benthic** and **planktonic** animals such as nematodes (round worms), oligochaetes (earthworms), molluscs, aquatic insects and various crustaceans (amphipods, copepods, etc.).

3 Exploitation

3.1 *Overview*

Natural colonies of *Procambarus clarkii* are exploited quite extensively in the USA (Louisiana), in Spain (Andalusia) and in Kenya (Lake Naivasha). Farming is most developed in the USA (more than 90 per cent of world production). In Louisiana in 1986, some 50 000 hectares of ponds produced 500 kg/ha annually, while in neighbouring Texas 7400 hectares produced 1000 kg/ha per year.

In other regions where the species is found in great numbers it is looked on as a pest – in Japan, Hawaii and California, for example. Its burrowing habits threaten irrigation schemes, and proliferation is not controlled by fishing since there is no tradition of eating crayfish in these countries.

The exploitation of natural populations must be examined in the light of the local hydrological cycle, to which it is closely connected. The examples given below involve distinct hydrological situations.

USA

In Louisiana, for instance, the hydrographic network of the Atchafalaya basin stretches over a swamp area 40 km wide and 160 km long, draining 30 per cent of the discharge of the Mississippi. The most important crayfish zone lies in the centre of the basin, where yearly fluctuations can reach 5 metres or more. The low zones are flooded by the late autumn and early winter rains.

The berried (egg-carrying) females come out of the holes and release the young in these areas. During river flooding in spring, the crayfish of that year grow rapidly and are abundantly fished in April, May and June, when they are 8 to 11 cm long. Access to production areas and fishing itself depend on the water level; the best catches always coincide with years of persistent late winter and spring floods (two out of five years on average). Annual harvests range between 10 000 and 50 000 tonnes, of which about 1100 and

900 tonnes were exported to Sweden in 1987 and 1988 respectively, and less than 100 tonnes to the rest of Europe.

Spain

In Spain, in the crayfish zone of the Guadalquivir rice basin, the hydrological cycle is controlled artificially to allow spring sowing, followed by paddy flooding, and then drainage in preparation for the autumn harvest. The crayfish multiply in the rice basins, in the irrigation canals and swamps around Seville where the species (less than 500 kg) was introduced in 1973 and 1974.

When the crayfish habitats are covered by water in the spring, the **ovigerous** mothers come out with the young; many adults are caught at this point but most of the harvesting takes place in the autumn when the paddy fields are drained. Here the farmer is not rearing crayfish: he does not develop his ricefields in order to farm them nor does he, generally speaking, harvest this production, which is left to local fishermen. Annual yields are about 5000 tonnes (Habsburgo-Lorena in J. Huner); the harvests are badly affected by drought and by the decrease in the acreage devoted to rice-growing.

Since its acclimatisation in Andalusia, *Procambarus clarkii* has, by natural migration and human propagation, considerably extended its distribution zone in the Spanish peninsula, particularly in the province of La Mancha. It has even established itself in the great rivers of the north, such as the Ebro, and is now exploited on a commercial basis throughout the country, which became France's main source of crayfish in 1987.

Kenya

Since its introduction at about the same time as in Spain, *Procambarus clarkii* has become widespread but is fished commercially only in Lake Naiwasha, by cooperative organisations.

Wet and dry seasons are clearly delineated so the water level drops sharply and regularly, although the lake never dries up completely. The berried females come out of the holes at the onset of the rainy season; the young grow fast and harvesting lasts from January to June, well before the dry season, when the level begins to drop.

Despite the presence of many aquatic birds, with a range of feeding habits, as well as several predatory fish species including the black bass *Micropterus salmoides*, the crayfish population is dense, thanks to the protection of thick layers of aquatic plants which grow on the banks during low water. The yearly marketable catch is between 400 and 500 tonnes.

China

Procambarus clarkii was introduced into China, probably from Japan, in early 1940. Since then, it has spread to 10 provinces where it is commonly found in waterways, ponds and irrigation systems.

The official statistics show that approximately 2000 tonnes are fished every year and the prospects for increased production through the simplest rearing methods are excellent. However, exploitation of the species is restricted by the lack of tradition of crayfish farming as well as by the damage done to irrigation networks by the species' burrowing.

The main crayfish production centre is in Hubei province where fish farmers catch small quantities in carp ponds, using nets and traps. Carp are not carnivorous as a rule and limited numbers of crayfish can thrive in the same ponds. Fish farmers still look on the crayfish as a pest in spawning grounds and rearing pools and use pesticides to keep their numbers as low as possible.

France

Introduced in different places at different times, the species is being studied very carefully in the Sarcelles pond, near Paris, where it is actively fished from May to November.

The crayfish are caught with hooks and lines by fishermen who have become specialists in the job.

The catches from this small two-hectare pond vary between 1 and 2.1 tonnes a year. The crayfish are eaten mainly by local inhabitants, many of whom are of Asian, West Indian and African extraction.

3.2 *Fishing*

Harvesting and transporting crayfish raises problems, both in the natural environment and in rearing pools. These difficulties are therefore analysed irrespective of where the crayfish are caught.

Catching gear

The crayfish are harvested almost exclusively by means of non-baited traps (see figures 12, 13 and 14). The most widely used material in the USA is chicken wire with 1.3 to 1.9 cm hexagonal meshing, often covered with black plastic to prolong its life. In Spain and in Kenya, nylon netting is used, while Spanish fishermen seem to prefer eel traps.

The net is cylindrical, about 2 metres long and 0.5 metres in diameter. The frame consists of hoops dividing the net into compartments, each with a funnel-like opening leading down to the bottom of the net where the catch accumulates. One or two wings, placed at right angles to the current, guide the crayfish towards the trap entrance which faces downstream. Whichever trap is used, at least one inlet must face downstream if there is a current.

Fig 12   *Collapsible, double entry Scandinavian trap*

Fig 13   *Triple entry trap*
(photo: Jay Huner)

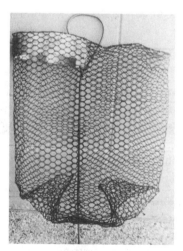

Fig 14   *Double entry trap*
with upper opening emerging

In natural fishing grounds, the trap must be completely submerged and rest horizontally on the bottom, because of the depth of the water. It must therefore be closed by some kind of hatch through which the catch can be removed or the bait renewed.

In aquaculture, depth seldom exceeds 0.5 m; the trap is placed vertically on the bottom, the upper end emerges, while the entrances to the trap are at its base. The captured crayfish can climb up and out of the water at the top end of the trap, where a circular metal-polished stopper prevents them from escaping. The open end allows the trap to be emptied quickly and the bait renewed. Since the aquatic environment is often rich in organic matter and, depending on the temperature, deficient in dissolved oxygen, the contraption is particularly useful because it allows the crayfish to make up for a lack of oxygen in the water by atmospheric breathing, thus avoiding the risk of death by asphyxiation. This is not so in deep waters without oxygen, where fishing is not feasible.

FISHING

Catching crayfish is easy since the main piece of equipment is an inexpensive trap which anyone can make by using:
- chicken wire
- iron reinforcing rods
- binding wire
- a bottle to make openings
- wire-cutters.

The traps are baited with fish of no commercial value.

Generally, active devices are not used for two main reasons. An active trap catches all crayfish indiscriminately, whether at the intermoult, premoult or moult stage; those at the premoult and moult stages are weak and are killed very easily. As they do not feed and seldom leave their burrows, they are unlikely to get trapped in a **non-baited device**. In addition, the crayfish environment is generally cluttered with waste that precludes a **dredge** or trawl track.

In Louisiana, however, a high-voltage, low-amp electrified **trawl net** has now appeared. An **anode** at the front of the boat and a **cathode** at the rear create a magnetic field on the **bow**; the crayfish rise to the surface and are caught by the trawl. Using this method, Louisiana crayfish farmers catch large quantities of soft-shelled crayfish which are now much in demand and fetch a high price.

In France, poachers make small hauls in coastal aquatic herbariums from which they remove the marketable crayfish.

Baits

In the USA, the traps are traditionally baited with unsaleable fish, the most popular being clupeids, catostomids and cyprinids. The extent of crayfish fishing in the South has led to the manufacture of artificial baits. The composition of these baits is identical to that of fish feed, but with less fish meal and other animal flours. The efficiency of these baits increases when the ambient temperature rises above 20°C, probably owing to the more rapid bacterial de-

Fig 15   *Spanish trap (photo: P. J. Laurent)*

Fig 16   *Layout of Spanish traps (photo: P. J. Laurent)*

composition of the cereal by-products and the ensuing release of attractive substances.

Spanish fishermen do not use bait. The crayfish are caught in the traps as they travel against the stream. The wings of the net at the trap entrance guide the animals towards the snare.

In France, in natural environments, fishermen with lines use meat baits.

Fishing boats and vehicles

Fishermen use ordinary fishing boats to catch crayfish in natural sites. In zones with high crayfish yields, the boats have been modified in order to increase fishing efficiency, owing to the high cost of manpower.

In Louisiana, for example, low-draught, rectangular, aluminium boats are used. They are powered by an outboard engine, fitted to the lower stern, and equipped with a long shaft and an anti-clogging propeller. They can explore shallow waters. One man pilots the craft while another drops or lifts the traps.

The 'Cajun Combine' is a kind of flat-bottomed barge with an **inboard** air-cooled 8 hp engine: this drives a notched wheel by water transmission. The wheel, operating on the swamp bed, guides, pulls or pushes the boat. Perched on a raised seat, controlling all the operations with a set of pedals, one operator is able to catch the crayfish.

Also on the market is a 4-wheel-drive vehicle, a modified paddy sprayer which moves along the banks; it is an efficient means of

Fig 17 *Cajun fishing boat (photo: J. Arrignon)*

Fig 18   *Motorboat with a notched wheel (photo: J. F. Martin)*

catching crayfish provided water depth is constant and the banks are of hard clay able to withstand its weight.

These systems have been developed in the USA because the production ponds are normally about 20 hectares in area and 50 to 100 traps must be set per hectare. Depending on the season and the abundance of crayfish, the traps may have to be lifted every 6 to 8 hours, although they are usually checked every 24 hours.

3.3   *Rearing*

Monoculture

Procambarus clarkii is successfully reared in the south of the USA by introducing permanent colonies which multiply by themselves in shallow pools, between 0.25 and 0.50 m deep. Intensive farming in semi-closed or closed systems is technically feasible but not commercially viable.

Rearing as practised in Louisiana is the model which has been transposed to other regions. The new ponds are stocked in late spring, when adults are plentiful and cheap. Population density varies from 20 to 100 kg/ha depending on the availability or otherwise of shelters, and the presence of indigenous crayfish populations. These are common in most swampy districts in Louisiana.

After several weeks under water, the pond is slowly emptied and the crayfish burrow holes in the bottom, above the low-water mark. Rice or suitable herbaceous cover plants can then be sown; reeds or other fast-growing plants are also acceptable. Plant biomass, expressed as dry matter, should be in the region of two to four tonnes per hectare.

In mid-autumn, the pond is flooded and the berried crayfish rise to the surface. The vegetation starts to rot and forms a sort of infusion rich in bacteria, providing the basis of the animal's food chain. Initially, mating may take place mainly in one pond but each of the

Fig 19 *Unloading crayfish packed in bags (photo: J. Arrignon)*

Fig 20 *Fishing* P. clarkii *with a line (photo: J. Arrignon)*

Fig 21 *Extensive rearing in open ponds (Louisiana, USA). Natural plant cover and the addition of hay bales here and there to reduce* **biochemical oxygen demand (BOD)** *immediately after filling up (photo: Jay Huner)*

Fig 22 *Procambarus hatchery (SLU, Lafayette, La, USA). There are 3 cm of water and each tube is covered with a mesh or fine plastic grid (photo: Jay Huner)*

26

ponds will eventually have a population spawning young throughout the autumn and into the winter. The latter are recognised by their **cohorts** that follow at intervals of two or three weeks and are essential if the pond is to meet the potential level of crayfish production in the region, i.e. 2500 to 3500 kg/ha. However, owing to many difficulties, including significant economic problems, the average annual production in Louisiana is about 700 kg/ha.

Harvesting can begin in mid-November, when the crayfish retained from the previous season have eaten abundantly and have finished growing. As a rule, fishing ends in mid-February, when the year's young begin to reach their marketable full-length size of 7 to 9 cm. In some cases fishing may last until early June if profits justify the work involved, although usually it ends in May when the pools are drained and the cycle described above is repeated.

Further north, fishing is postponed until the late spring and summer since growth is stopped by low winter temperatures. In central Arkansas for example, serious harvesting does not begin until early May and lasts until July, whereas in northern Ohio, it can be delayed until July. Although experience in higher latitudes is limited, it is obvious that the ponds must not be fully drained in winter because of the risk that the ground might freeze to below the bottom of the burrows. However, changes in the behaviour of *Procambarus clarkii* were observed in France during the two severe winters of 1984/1985 and 1985/1986, when the animals burrowed deeper to escape

Fig 23 *Crayfish stocked in a moulting pond. Note the animal density and the water supplied by spraying (photo: Jay Huner)*

Fig 24   *Tanks for purging the crayfish before selling (photo: Jay Huner)*

the gradual hardening of the ground. Drainage in summer is also ruled out because this is the growing season in cold climates. Farm crops must be sown in the early spring, before the ponds are fully flooded in preparation for the hatching and maturing of the young crayfish emerging from the burrows.

Rearing soft-shelled crayfish

Soft-shelled crayfish are now a successful market product in the USA. They can be fished during either moulting or premoulting. In the first case, the use of a traditional trawl net and drag-seine in ponds full of plant debris involves considerable work, and the increase in efficiency is not justified by the added value of the product; in these cases, a powered dredge is more efficient.

Soft-shelled crayfish can also be produced using specimens caught during premoulting, then kept in tanks until they leave their shells. Early premoulting crayfish must be fed to avoid cannibalism and must first be sorted depending on their specific moulting stage.

Mixed farming

Crayfish can be reared in association with the growing of plants such as rice, soya or even with fish, although rotation with rice is the most typical and noteworthy commercial venture.

Combined production of rice and crayfish

Although rice is grown in flooded fields, crayfish do not like living in these conditions because the water is shallow and therefore too warm in summer. In south-western Louisiana and in neighbouring south-eastern Texas, two rotations in the year are usually preferred.

During the first rotation, rice is sown in mid-spring and the paddies are stocked with crayfish when the water level is raised in order to kill the weeds. The crayfish burrow into the banks as the temperature rises. The use of pesticides must be avoided, although fungicides and some herbicides are tolerated. If an insecticide is needed, choose one with low toxicity and only apply it when plant cover is well developed.

The rice is harvested in August and the field is flooded again in September or October, this time for the crayfish. It is advisable to raise the bunds to increase the depth of the rice basins to 30 cm instead of the 10 to 15 cm usually required for rice-growing. Harvesting begins when the plentiful supply of crayfish justifies the work involved and as long as catches are profitable. Fishing usually ends in early May, after the rice planting. The drained fields are often sown by aeroplane; this is a method which considerably reduces the cost of land preparation. The cycle can then begin again.

An alternative is to harvest the crayfish until the end of May, when the paddies are drained for soya planting. The rice/crayfish/soya cycle will then begin once again the following spring after winter drainage and before stocking up again with crayfish. Note that soya stubble does not produce enough waste to meet the needs of a crayfish population in production.

BEWARE OF CHEMICAL SUBSTANCES

More than fish, crayfish are sensitive to chemicals, such as:
- pesticides used to control insects
- certain weedkillers.

Ask the engineer, technician or supervisor for advice before applying chemical substances on a pond or paddy containing crayfish.

Alternate rearing of prawns and crayfish

Rotating prawns (*Macrobrachium rosenbergii*) and crayfish (*Procambarus clarkii*) can be worthwhile. In Louisiana, crayfish grow from mid-October to mid-May and prawns from mid-May to mid-October. Trials show that the alternate and consecutive rearing of the two crustaceans does not affect their original output and therefore markedly increases the productivity of a stretch of water.

In plots flooded under a metre of water, adult crayfish were introduced with densities of between 60 and 180 kg/ha. Rice as a fodder plant was sown in May, at the rate of 120 kg/ha, and, early in July, juvenile prawns (0.02 g/unit) were fattened there at the rate of 17 500 per hectare; in some plots the prawns were given commercial feed daily.

The prawns were harvested in October and the crayfish were trapped daily from late January to mid-May. The prawn harvest amounted to 295 kg/ha, and that of crayfish averaged 983 kg/ha with a maximum of 1683 kg/ha.

Rearing beef and crayfish together

Cattle are generally reared in rotation from pasture to pasture, each with a water hole. By making some improvements, the water holes can be adapted for rearing crayfish.

Trials in this connection were carried out in Arkansas (USA). An 80-are rectangular basin, 15 to 75 cm deep, was filled with water from autumn until early the following spring and stocked with crayfish (mostly *Procambarus clarkii*) at the rate of 30 000 units measuring 2.5 cm. The harvest, affected by a prolonged drought, yielded 135 kg.

The experiment is worth trying because the fact that the water hole is fertilised by the cattle dung and the livestock is supplied with hay stimulates crayfish production. Since the livestock must have water anyway, development costs are split and set off between the two productions – cattle and crayfish.

The experiment was inspired by the African practice of rearing tilapia in lakes and storage pools designed to water wandering cattle.

3.4 *Problems connected with rearing*

Water quality

Water quality is the only major problem connected with the rearing of *Procambarus clarkii* as it is practised today. Basically it stems from the **trophic** needs of crayfish which require an environment rich in plant debris and organic detritus. In the space of two weeks after they are filled with water, crayfish ponds show signs of serious disoxygenation caused by the **biological oxygen demand** (BOD) of rotting vegetation. At a later stage, when the temperature drops below

20°C, the dissolved oxygen content rises above the favourable 3 ppm mark, only to drop again in early spring when the water warms up.

These difficulties may then be compounded by the appearance of **algal blooms**, dense filamentous algae that are resistant to cold. The algae dramatically increase BOD when they die.

Civil engineering offers a solution. During construction, the ponds must be laid out lengthways, orientated in the direction of the prevailing winds, so that by thorough mixing, water circulation and aeration can be improved. Longitudinal dykes can be built every 50 metres. In addition, when the pond is drained, half its vegetation can be cut and stacked to prevent it from rotting too quickly; the other half is left standing to help the crayfish rise to the surface by climbing up the stems.

If day temperatures exceed 26°C, the filling of the ponds can be delayed until the temperature drops or they need only be half-filled, in order to prevent water dilution or recirculation. Mechanical airing, as applied in other forms of aquaculture, is unworkable for rearing *Procambarus clarkii* in pools.

However, it is always worth adding good quality water or recirculating the water in the pond, aerated so as to raise its dissolved oxygen content. In this case, it is advisable to carry out the operation two weeks after the ponds have been filled in the autumn, or as often as necessary in the spring. Water must enter the pond through a set of three or four vertical distributors with openings narrowing gradually from 1.8 to 0.6 cm in diameter in order to ensure oxygen saturation. Pumping capacity must be designed to permit water renewal every four days – i.e. approximately 1000 litres per second per hectare.

When underground water likely to contain high levels of hydrogen sulphide and/or ferro compounds is used, the water should be distributed by filtering it through materials such as hay to avoid accidents. Surface water should also be checked for agricultural pesticides.

WATCH THE TEMPERATURE OF THE WATER

When crayfish are put into a rearing pool, the temperature must not exceed 25°C.

Daily variables and how they affect catches

Dissolved oxygen, water temperature, atmospheric pressure, wind force and velocity strongly influence crayfish catching. In Louisiana, these variables can trigger wide discrepancies: 32 per cent of yield variations are explained by these daily variables, of which:

- 85.3 per cent by the variation in water temperature as well as by crayfish density in the pool
- 7.1 per cent by the lunar phase
- 5 per cent by rainfall
- 3 per cent by the onset of cold weather.

Catches therefore increase considerably when water temperature rises above 18°C, and also during afternoon rains. They drop with the full moon and during a cold spell.

This information can help producers to calculate probable fishing results according to weather changes and to bear in mind that yields are highest with water temperatures between 20 and 25°C.

Predators

The major invertebrate predators, which prey more especially on the juveniles, are aquatic insects (nymphs and adults) and crustaceans – crabs and crayfish themselves.

Amphibians, such as the bullfrog, are also dangerous predators. Sea snakes, in particular, and crocodiles, occasionally, feed on crayfish.

Herons, egrets and ibis are also dangerous; crayfish form 90 to 95 per cent of the daily food intake of the Louisiana crowned heron (large billed). They form 50 to 60 per cent and 45 to 50 per cent respectively of the daily rations of the large billed ibis and of the small blue heron.

Finally, some mammals, such as raccoons, minks, otters, opossums and muskrats, have a taste for crayfish.

Procambarus clarkii provides part of the food intake of many fish, for example black bass, pumpkinseed, catfish and eel. When rearing crayfish, producers must be sure to bear in mind this aspect of predation.

Fish living in swamps with high BOD, such as catfish, *Ictalurus* spp., *Lepomis cyanellus* (or green sunfish, known in French-speaking Canada as the 'crapet vert'), can withstand very low oxygen content and can easily invade and contaminate pools if steps are not taken to kill individuals which slip in or manage to survive in holes after drainage: these can hold out until the pools are filled up again. These fish are usually eliminated by **rotenone** poisoning (two to five per cent), with a three to five ppm dose.

Another source of predation is the entry of the same predatory fish when pools are filled without the inlet being fitted with a grating, or if filling occurs when embankments are overtopped during a spate flow. In both cases, the crayfish suffer from predation which will last until the pond is drained and then treated with rotenone.

Cessation of growth

Cessation of growth can become a problem since there is no means of effectively controlling the number of crayfish in a pond. Ponds are restocked annually by their own population, which maintains itself. Relative densities and growth rates of different cohorts can be monitored but at the present time the only way of reducing density is to remove the largest crayfish regularly with the help of traps, thus letting the next, smaller cohort replace the previous one.

Cessation of growth is inevitable until the large crayfish have been eliminated. The speed with which the aquatic vegetation disappears is usually proportional to crayfish density and if it disappears before the spring, additional feed will be needed.

Spoilt hay is the most common source of additional feed. It can come in the form of bales made up in the pool before it is filled with water, or brought in from outside. The quantities required have not been determined with precision but they must never be greater than 1000 to 2000 kg/ha at any time, and the rate of consumption and effects of this rotting material must be carefully followed up.

4 Problems

4.1 Competition

In the centre of the USA, *Procambarus clarkii* often settles spontaneously in fish-farming ponds intended for production of **fish fry**. Predator fish are usually put in to eliminate the crayfish because these compete with the fish fry for space and food, although some fish farmers find it profitable to leave them and market them later. Combined rearing of crayfish and fish is more successful when the fry are put into ponds already stocked with crayfish, because these eat fish eggs in spawning grounds.

In fish-farming lakes and ponds, crayfish damage the fishing nets and more specifically the **trammel nets**, from which it is difficult to disentangle them. They also spoil the pleasure of amateur fishermen by snatching the bait intended for fish.

4.2 Destruction of habitats

Adverse environmental impacts, both direct and indirect, have occurred as a result of introduction of *Procambarus clarkii*. Of these, habitat destruction has given the greatest cause for concern, Introductions within the USA have caused marked reductions – or even elimination – of native aquatic plants in some areas (Feminella and Resh 1989). Adapted to temporary drought conditions as well as to extremes of temperatures, *Procambarus clarkii* finds the humidity or appropriate **thermal gradient** it needs to survive by burrowing.

Whenever the water level of a pond, lake, river or canal drops, *Procambarus clarkii* burrows to search for optimal living conditions. Likewise, in intense heat or cold, the crayfish starts burrowing until it reaches a suitable ambient temperature. In the process, it tunnels through banks, dykes and levees, settles under slabs, undermines beds, causes subsidence and collapse, connects ponds that should have remained impermeable and drains canals or rice fields.

Even the foundations of hydraulic structures may be at risk. In France, for instance, *Procambarus clarkii* has worked its way under sluice-gates and dams at Sarcelles communal pond, between the cement and clay interface (Arrignon and Blin 1990). This causes recurrent, seasonal damage the cost of which owners and rural farmers have to bear. These may or may not be insured; they may receive compensation from public funds normally reserved for damage to crops by wild animals such as stags and boars, something which is not infrequent in Japan and Spain.

Indirect impacts of introductions of *Procambarus clarkii* have also been recorded. Increasing fishing activity has caused incidental damage to other animal communities, particularly amphibians (Delibes and Adrian 1987), whilst attempts to erradicate the species through heavy use of pesticides in countries such as Portugal have led to problems with water quality.

> The red swamp crayfish digs holes.
> This is one reason why some countries ban live imports of *Procambarus clarkii*.

These facts must be borne in mind, particularly in dry countries where water is scarce and precious, where all forms of agriculture require irrigation and drainage with resultant variations in water levels that would necessarily lead to *Procambarus clarkii* burrowing, and its ensuing damage.

The wandering character of the species encourages it to migrate over considerable distances in search of the appropriate living conditions and therefore gradually to invade ever-wider areas, thus increasing the hazards of its presence. Since the introduction of red swamp crayfish to the area around Seville in Spain in the early 1970s, for example, it has spread rapidly throughout much of the Iberian peninsula.

Almost all successful introductions of red swamp crayfish have been to agricultural areas where extensive irrigation systems are in place. However, in most cases the introductions have brought little economic or social benefit. Moreover, even in cases where the introduction and acclimatisation of *Procambarus clarkii* seems justified, the risks identified above should clearly be borne in mind, and provision must be made for installations and an aquacultural or husbandry policy geared to the behaviour of the species as described in section 2.5.

4.3 *Pathology*

Susceptibility of *Procambarus clarkii*

DISEASES

At the present time the rearing or natural biological cycle of *Procambarus clarkii* is not affected by any disease, although even healthy individuals may be germ-carriers. Some diseases should nevertheless be mentioned.

Bacterial exoskeleton disease leads to exoskeleton erosion caused by bacteria which attack the chitin and cause the organism to be invaded by pathogenic germs. This is a potential threat only to slow-growing animals, since the harmful germs are discarded with each moulting.

Bacteria of the digestive system may produce harmful **exotoxins** when crayfish live in confinement, in the absence of water circulation which is sufficient to prevent proliferation. High concentrations of bacteria of the genus *Vibrio* have been detected in populations living in waters above 27°C.

Protozoa, external commensals, may cover crayfish gills that do not moult, thus contributing to deaths caused by a drop in oxygen exchanges.

Microsporidia, bearers of the porcelain disease in crustaceans, have recently been identified in *Procambarus clarkii* but no epidemic comparable to that which has taken such a heavy toll of Australian or European crayfish has been observed.

None of the helminths are held responsible for reduced catches although their presence may affect the quality of the muscles eaten and at least one genus, *Paragonimus*, is potentially pathogenic for man (*P. westmani*, in Japan) as well as for cats and dogs (*P. kellicotti*, in the USA). Cooking eliminates this danger.

Formalin, malachite green and sodium chloride, used to control external parasites, bacteria and diseases in fish, are efficient in concentrations used in fish farming.

The species is resistant to the parasitic fungus *Aphanomyces astaci*, but it can act as a vector and contaminate European crayfish and those in the southern hemisphere. These have no known resistance to the disease, which is responsible for wiping out many European fisheries.

Branchiobdellid worms are often found in large numbers on *Procambarus clarkii*. White in colour, 1 cm long, these small annelid worms are considered to be **ectocommensal**; they lay small eggs on the shell and are unpleasant themselves when present in large numbers. *Corixid hemipterans*, known as 'water boatmen' in the USA, also lay vast quantities of eggs on the animals' shell after moultings; they can make the crayfish unattractive to look at, but are not harmful. They teem more particularly in warm waters.

Procambarus clarkii, vector of disease

The permeability of live crayfish import markets enhances the risk of propagating pathogenic germs. Generally speaking, the resistant vector species manifest no symptoms that could bar their entry. *Procambarus clarkii*, like the other species on the American continent, is one such species. As already mentioned, its introduction can lead to that of known or unknown germs, which may cause severe **epizootic diseases** in local crayfish stocks.

Consequently, all sorts of measures have been envisaged at State level, in European countries in particular, and have been implemented in certain cases. One set of measures demanded keeping imported live crayfish in **quarantine** before marketing. However, these measures failed to be implemented because of the infrastructure required, the immobilisation of appropriate sites and the cost of the facilities.

Regulations have been drawn up banning the import of *Procambarus clarkii* under its **vernacular name** of 'red crayfish' or 'red-legged crayfish', the name commonly given to *Astacus astacus*, a European crayfish reputed for the quality of its flesh and its delicate flavour.

Apparently the most effective measure is to ban the sale of live crayfish, whatever the species, and to limit imports to tails, or even to whole cooked or frozen animals and pre-packed culinary preparations.

5 Marketing

5.1 *Packing and storing*

Once caught, the crayfish are stored in loosely woven bags (of the kind used for transporting vegetables), which can take about 20 kg of the crustaceans. The bags must be kept in the shade and in a humid atmosphere but away from the water lying in the bottom of the boat, which is usually fouled by motor-fuel. If the shells are thin and fragile, as is the case when crayfish are growing rapidly, care must be taken to put fewer animals into the sacks to avoid large numbers of animals being crushed and killed by their own weight.

In Louisiana it is customary to transfer the bagged crayfish to cold rooms where the temperature is maintained between 4 and 6°C. Normally, they travel in the bags at this temperature. Mortality is less than five per cent after five days, if the bags are kept damp and – because of the danger of crushing – stored side by side rather than one on top of another.

Fig 25   *Storing crayfish in bags in a factory (photo: J.F. Martin)*

Fig 26   *Cleaning and sorting crayfish in a factory (photo: J.F. Martin)*

The use of purging tanks to clean and store crayfish is not wide-spread in the USA. They exist only in places with a sizeable market for live animals and where high-quality products command a good price. It takes 24 to 48 hours for crayfish to empty their digestive tract; this can be done by submitting the animals to a fog emitted through ventilation ducts, or by immersion in a tank. The materials used for the construction of the storage tanks must not be toxic (certain plastic materials must therefore be avoided).

Purging systems are compulsory by law in Spain. It is claimed that purged crayfish travel better than non-purged ones; it must be noted, however, that losses due to purging may be as high as 20 per cent.

PRECAUTIONS DURING TRANSPORT

When transporting live crayfish in bags out of water, do not stack the bags one on top of another, otherwise the crayfish underneath will be crushed to death.

5.2 *Processing*

Crayfish are sold either alive or prepared. In the USA, small animals with a total length of 2 to 7 cm are mainly sold off as **bait**. The larger ones are marketed for human consumption. Crayfish produced in Spain and Kenya are handled in the same way.

Freezing

The traditional product consists of freshly boiled whole crayfish; this can be deep-frozen and delivered to distant markets, as is the case for the European market. The crayfish can be quickly frozen when still alive, and boiled later without thawing, since **proteolytic enzymes** of the hepatopancreas spoil the quality of the meat if they are activated by thawing.

Fig 27   *Shelling the tails before packing (photo: J.F. Martin)*

Fig 28   *Processing shells and debris to make flour (photo: J.F. Martin)*

Deep-frozen crayfish are not yet in wide demand although they are a sound, potentially competitive product. Louisiana is the only place where a crayfish processing industry has been established in order to preserve the surplus stocks left over from the fresh product market. This is a growth sector and cooked dishes such as fried crayfish tails, crayfish soup and braised crayfish are becoming more popular in the USA as well as in other countries, of which Spain is a recent example.

Abdominal muscles are shelled by hand after the animals are boiled live for five to ten minutes. Approximately 15 per cent of the initial weight is recovered. An extra five per cent is saved by retaining the hepatopancreas which is much in demand on traditional Louisiana markets but far less elsewhere, the reason being that this part of the body cannot be deep-frozen with the muscles since it becomes spoilt very quickly.

The muscles to be deep-frozen must be plunged into a weak solution of **citric acid** (one to two per cent) to prevent them from turning bluish-purple as a result of oxidation. Crayfish tails are also used as ingredients to enhance frozen dishes. As a rule, no attempt is made to remove the flesh in the claws.

Preparation of soft-shelled crayfish

Small soft-shelled crayfish are a traditional bait, highly prized by USA fishermen, and the centre of a flourishing trade. Note, too, that large soft-shelled crayfish, already very popular in Louisiana, are now being marketed and command prices 10 to 15 times higher than those of hard crayfish. Frying is the most usual method of preparation but the food can also be served grilled or cooked in the oven along the lines of the traditional dishes made from blue crab when it is soft. Before preparing the dish, the hard gastroliths must be removed because they could damage the eater's teeth.

Processing waste

The technology for manufacturing protein-rich flours and extracting carotenoid from the residues left after shelling is gradually taking shape in Louisiana. Two recycling factories meet the needs of more than 80 recognised crayfish processing plants. They produce plain flour, rich in proteins and with a high calcium content. The fresh residues make an excellent enriching agent and can be used as fertilisers.

5.3 *Gastronomy*

Food value

With only about 100 calories per kilogram, crayfish meat is a valuable food in nutritional terms, because of its low fat content and its significant levels of protein, iron, calcium and vitamins.

> **CRAYFISH MEAT IS A RICH FOOD WHICH GOES WELL WITH RICE.**

Calcium	770 mg/kg
Phosphorus	2013 mg/kg
Iron	15 mg/kg
Vitamin B	
Thiamin	1.1 mg/kg
Riboflavin	0.42 mg/kg
Niacin	19.4 mg/kg
Proteins	146 g/kg
Lipids	5.1 g/kg
Carbohydrates	11.9 g/kg

Crayfish meat fibres, being shorter than those found in other animal meats, are very digestible.

Everyday dishes served with rice

Rice and crayfish form a natural culinary association, much as rice and fish and other crustaceans in the tropics. Local recipes based on rice will therefore be a help when preparing dishes in which crayfish is the choice ingredient: curries, rice with seed sauces, paella and caldero. The crayfish can even be served with hard wheat semolinas or manioc (cassava).

Acadian recipes

In Louisiana (the top-ranking American State as regards world crayfish production), *Procambarus clarkii* is an ingredient in the following traditional Acadian and Creole specialities:

Crayfish risotto with saffron (six servings)
- 1/2 cup chopped onion
- 1 tablespoon butter or margarine
- 1 cup dry rice with saffron

- 1/3 cup white wine
- 1 1/2 cups flageolets
- 200 g crayfish tails cooked and peeled
- 1/4 teaspoon each of salt and pepper
- 1/4 cup cream
- 1/4 cup grated gruyère or parmesan cheese
- 2 cups chicken stock
- 1 teaspoon lemon juice

Melt the butter in a large frying pan or casserole, add the onions and cook over low heat. Add the rice and saffron, stirring for 2 to 3 minutes. Add the wine, stirring until it is absorbed. Add a cup of stock, stirring frequently until it is absorbed. Continue stirring, gradually adding the remaining stock and 3 cups of water until the liquid has been absorbed and the rice cooked (25–30 minutes). The mixture should be of a creamy consistency. Add the remaining ingredients and cook for about 2 minutes, stirring all the time.

Composition of each helping : 258 calories, 11.7 g proteins, 7.2 g fat, 33.3 g carbohydrates, 543 mg sodium and 44 mg cholesterol.

Crayfish Jambalaya (six servings)
- 2 tablespoons oil
- 1 cup minced onion
- 1/2 cup minced celery
- 1 1/4 cup rice
- 2 cloves of garlic (crushed)
- 1/2 tin tomato sauce
- parsley, salt and pepper
- 3 to 4 cups water
- 1 tablespoon flour
- 1/2 cup chopped green peppers
- 1/2 cup minced green onions
- 2 1/2 cups peeled crayfish tails
- 500 g fresh tomatoes
- 1/4 teaspoon red pepper
- 1 1/2 cups chicken stock

In a large frying pan or casserole, make a roux with the oil and the flour. Add the onions, celery, garlic and peppers. Stir, mixing well. Add the rice, the crayfish tails and the remaining ingredients. Stir. Add the water. Bring to the boil and simmer for 20 minutes until the rice is soft and the liquid has evaporated. Adjust the seasoning.

Composition of each helping : 233 calories, 14.6 g proteins, 4.7 g fat, 32.3 g carbohydrates, 992 mg sodium and 61 mg cholesterol.

Braised crayfish (five servings)
- 125 g butter or margarine
- 1 cup chopped celery
- 2 cloves of garlic (crushed)
- 1/4 cup freshly chopped parsley
- 1 teaspoon salt
- 1/4 teaspoon red pepper or paprika to colour the dish
- 500 g peeled crayfish tails
- 2 tablespoons fecula (potato flour or other thickener)
- 1 cup chopped onions
- 1 cup chopped green peppers
- 1/4 cup chopped green onions
- 1 tin tomato sauce
- 1/2 teaspoon black pepper
- 3 cups hot cooked rice

Sauté the onions, celery, peppers and garlic in the butter or margarine until brown (5 minutes). Add 1/2 cup water, cover and simmer for 15 minutes (until the vegetables are cooked). Add the crayfish tails, the green onions and parsley, and stir. Mix the fecula in half a cup of water, pour over the dish, mix and season. Cover and cook a further 15 minutes, stirring if necessary. Serve hot over the hot rice.

Crayfish sauté (four servings)
- 1 kg peeled crayfish tails
- 1/4 cup butter
- 1/2 teaspoon salt
- 1 tablespoon lemon juice
- 1 tablespoon minced hot peppers (chilies)
- 1/2 cup chopped green onions
- 1 cup dry white wine
- 1/8 teaspoon pepper
- 3 tablespoons oil

Sauté the crayfish in the oil for 2 or 3 minutes. Add the butter and the onions, sautéing for a minute. Remove the crayfish. Add the wine to the butter-onion mixture and heat until the sauce thickens. Put back the crayfish, add the salt, pepper and lemon juice and cook, stirring for 1 to 2 minutes. Serve with hot rice, crackers, or tomatoes and broccoli.

Crayfish fritters (four servings)
- 500 g peeled crayfish tails
- 1 teaspoon salt
- 1/2 teaspoon yeast
- 2 eggs

- 1 tablespoon lemon juice
- 1 cup flour
- 1/2 teaspoon black pepper
- 1/4 teaspoon red pepper
- 1/2 cup powdered milk
- oil for frying

Mix the flour, yeast, salt and pepper in a bowl. In another bowl, beat the eggs, adding the milk and lemon juice; mix well. Dip the crayfish tails into the batter, then coat thoroughly in the prepared flour. Have the oil at the right temperature (390–400°C). Deep-fry the fritters until golden. Remove and drain, then serve very hot with tartare sauce or ketchup.

6 Freshwater prawns – introduction

The large freshwater prawn *Macrobrachium rosenbergii* (de Man) originally came from southeast Asia where it has been exploited for many years. It is traditionally fished in its natural habitat – estuaries, rivers, tropical lakes and rice channels.

The scientific name of the crayfish is *Macrobrachium rosenbergii* (de Man). It is referred to by a number of common names which – unfortunately – it shares with other crustaceans:

- the prawn in the Pacific
- the camaron in east Africa, the Indian Ocean, Cameroon
- the écrevisse z'habitant in Martinique
- the ouassou in Guadeloupe
- the langostino in Puerto Rico
- the freshwater prawn, Malaysian prawn or giant river prawn in the USA
- the missala in West Africa.

The French name used by the FAO means literally 'giant freshwater prawn', a logical name since the crayfish and prawn found off European coasts both come from the same family of Palaemonids.

The commercial name which has recently come into use in France literally means 'blue Caribbean prawn'. For the purposes of simplification, the name 'giant freshwater prawn' or 'freshwater prawn' will be used in this manual.

Following successful experimental breeding in hatcheries at the end of the sixties, the species has been reared in many countries in the tropics (Fig. 29).

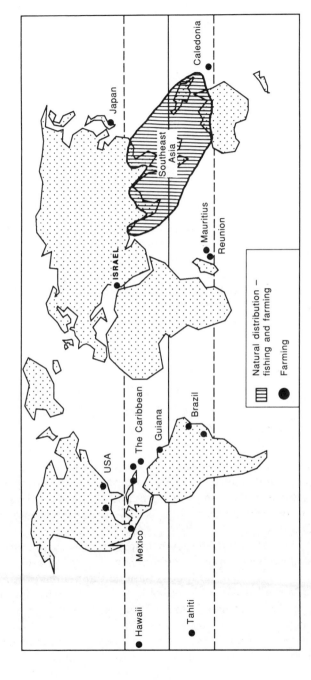

Fig 29 *Principal countries in the tropics catching and farming species of* Macrobrachium. *The hatched area indicates the region where the species is naturally found.*

7 Biology

7.1 Classification

The giant freshwater prawn is, like all prawns, a Natantia decapod crustacean of the Carides sub-order and Palaemonidae family. It is a member of the genus *Macrobrachium*, a genus of tropical crustaceans which lives in fresh or brackish water, and the species *rosenbergii*. The first broodstock was imported into Hawaii from Malaysia at the beginning of the 1960s. It was from this stock that the first giant freshwater prawns were reared outside the species' natural area. The progeny of this stock, known as 'anuenue', though very small in number (36), was used for starting all the farms outside this region, i.e. in the southern USA, Central America, Polynesia, the Caribbean, South America and the Indian Ocean.

7.2 Morphology

Figure 30 shows an adult male. Note the following:
- the cephalothorax bearing the antennae, eyes, mouth parts and five pairs of walking legs or pereopods (The second pair of legs, which are well developed especially in the male, end in strong claws.)
- a laterally flattened abdomen made up of six segments with appendages, the pleopods, which are used for swimming (The sixth segment carries the **uropods**, flattened appendages which form a blade used for moving quickly backwards or for flight. At the end of the abdomen is the telson, a pointed part with no appendages.)

Blue is the dominant colour, the claws and abdomen having the most pigment. Figure 31 shows how to distinguish easily between the freshwater prawn and the penaeid shrimp. In the freshwater prawn the **pleura** of the second abdominal segment overlap those of the first and third segments, while in the penaeid shrimp they

48

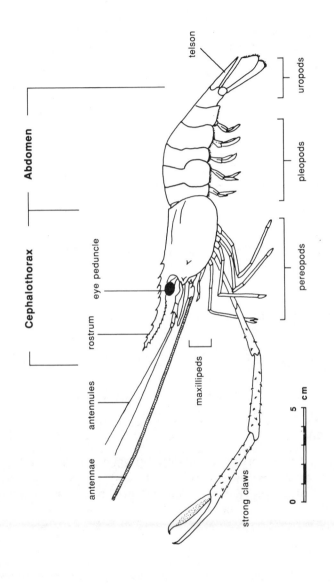

Fig 30   *Adult male* Macrobrachium rosenbergii

49

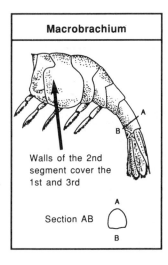
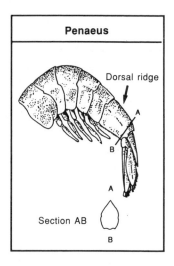

Fig 31   *Differences in the abdomen of a* Macrobrachium *and a* Penaeus

overlap each other like tiles on a roof. In addition, the last abdominal segment is round while that of penaeid prawn has a dorsal ridge.

In the freshwater prawn half the length of the body and 55 to 60 per cent of the total weight is taken up by the cephalothorax – hence the importance of finding markets which will take the whole animal.

7.3   *Physiology*

Like all crustaceans the giant freshwater prawn breathes through gills and grows by moulting several times.

Respiration

Respiration (the exchange of dissolved oxygen and carbon dioxide) takes place at the gills, which are on either side of the cephalothorax, under the carapace. Giant freshwater prawns maintain a current of water within the gill cavities to enable the distribution and exchange of gases.

Osmoregulation

During their lives giant freshwater prawns migrate several times between environments of different salinity. They live in brackish water during the larval stage; when adult they live in fresh water. Growth stops when salinity reaches 0.5 per cent. This ability to adapt to changes in concentrations in the surrounding environment is known as osmoregulation. Macrobrachia are hyperosmotic in relation to their natural environment.

Gill respiration, moulting and osmoregulation make the freshwater prawn very sensitive to water quality. Table 3 gives the optimal tolerance and growth limits for the freshwater prawn.

Table 3 Limits of tolerance and optimum values of the principal environmental factors for the freshwater prawn

Parameter	Lower limit	Optimum	Upper limit
Dissolved oxygen (mg/l)	1.5	saturation	
Temperature (°C)	18	28–32	36
pH	5.5	7–8	9.5
Hardness (mg/l $CaCO_3$ equivalent)		40–100	400

7.4 *Food*

Giant freshwater prawns are omnivorous and under natural conditions feed on aquatic products – vegetable waste, zooplankton and microscopic fauna living on the bottom (insect larvae, small worms and microorganisms).

FOOD
The natural food of the freshwater prawn is vegetable waste, plankton, insect larvae, small worms and microorganisms. When farmed commercially, manufactured feedstuffs are also supplied.

Natural food also plays an important part in farming, especially for young prawns. However, stocking densities are such that because of the rapid increase in the **biomass**, supplementary feed has to be provided to compensate for reduced supplies from impoverishment of the natural environment and to ensure continuing satisfactory growth of the entire stock.

7.5 *Reproduction and life cycle*

Young prawns can breed from about the fifth month. Mating takes place in fresh water between a dominant male with blue claws and a female which has just moulted. The genital pores are underneath

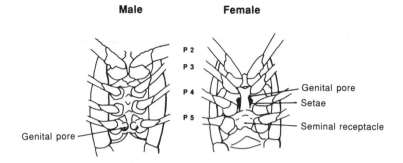

Male   **Female**

P 2
P 3
P 4
P 5

Genital pore
Setae
Seminal receptacle

Genital pore

Fig 32   *The thorax of a male and female seen from below showing the positions of the genital pores and seminal receptacle*

the body at the base of the third pair of legs in the female and of the fifth pair in the male (fig. 32). The male turns the female over and deposits a mass of sperm at the mouth of the genital pore. Eggs are therefore fertilised as soon as they are laid.

Spawning takes place some hours after mating. Between 5000 and 30 000 eggs, 0.25 mm in diameter, are produced, the number depending on the size of the female (about 350 to 500 eggs per gram body weight, with young females producing most eggs per unit body weight). The eggs are guided by the pleopods towards the brood chamber under the female's abdomen. Glands at these appendages secrete a gelatinous substance which binds the eggs together (Plate E). Incubation lasts 15 to 20 days depending on the temperature. The eggs are oxygenated and cleaned by the constant moving of the pleopods. They are yellow/orange when laid and gradually become darker until just before hatching, when they are grey.

Although growth, mating and the hatching of larvae take place in fresh water, larvae can only develop in water with a salinity of 1.0 to 1.4 per cent. Under natural conditions only larvae hatched in the lower reaches of rivers can develop since currents take them to the estuaries.

Growth

The newly-hatched larva measures 2 mm in length. Larval growth, which lasts from four to six weeks depending on water temperature, takes place in six stages, at the end of which the larva metamorphoses into a post-larva 10–15 mm long and weighing 10–12 mg. At metamorphosis, post-larvae go to the bottom, where they remain and feed. Post-larvae are virtually miniature adults since their morphology is the same. Growth follows an S curve, the rate depending

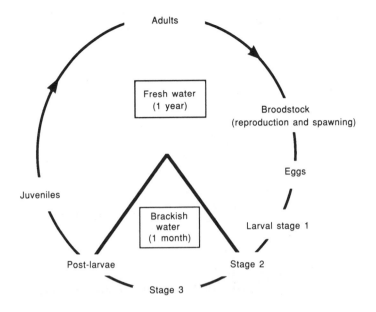

Fig 33   The life cycle of *Macrobrachium rosenbergii*

on ecological conditions such as temperature and the availability of food. After some days the young prawns, attracted by fresh water, move upstream where they spend their adult lives.

Macrobrachium rosenbergii is the largest *Macrobrachium* species after *M. carcinus* (a South American and Caribbean species). Males can weigh over 500 g in their natural environment; females are smaller. Figure 33 shows the **life cycle** of a freshwater prawn.

Migration

Larvae develop in brackish water. When they reach the juvenile stage, they go back to fresh water where they grow, mature and reproduce.

7.6   *Behaviour and social structure of farmed prawns*

If eggs are put into a pool and allowed to develop, the females will be seen to be practically all the same size after several months growth while males vary considerably. This marked variation in size is characteristic of the species. Figure 34 shows the difference in size distribution in a population of giant freshwater prawns and penaeids

Proportions (%)

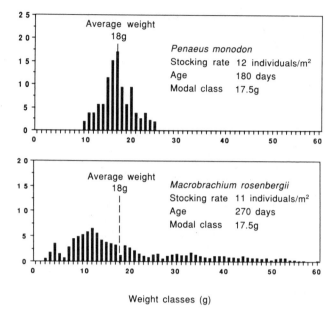

Weight classes (g)

Fig 34   *Comparison of populations of freshwater prawns and penaeids at identical average weights*

of the same average weight. The variation in giant freshwater prawns has a determining influence on farming methods, which try to exploit rather than merely to tolerate this characteristic.

Separate examination of the growth of both males and females shows that this variation in growth is found only among the males and that it is apparent from a very early age. It is based on two sorts of competition:

- **Competition for food**
  This is of relatively little importance in the younger stages, during which prawns feed mainly on natural food which is readily available. However, it is more important when they are larger, when food for cultured stock consists principally of manufactured pellets which are often not uniformly distributed and the size of which (2.5–2.5 mm in diameter) is more suitable for the larger animals.

- **Social competition**
  Some males reveal a very early tendency to aggression and exhibit a strong sense of territory. The other males soon conform to the patterns set by the dominant males.

Males are classified into three types or 'morphotypes' according to the claw colour and claw size in proportion to body size (Plate F):

- small males with whitish claws
- intermediate-sized males with orange claws
- large males with large blue claws.

These three male types play specific roles in the population.

Large blue-clawed males are dominant; they are responsible for most of the mating and are aggressive, using their claws to defend territories where females hide during reproduction. A territory is a depression in the ground where the females of a harem can hide at the critical stage of moulting. When females moult, which takes place less often than in males, their growth slows down and their bodies are often covered with algae, giving them a greenish colour.

Orange-clawed males are sub-dominant, i.e. they may become blue-clawed males at their next moult. They do not defend a territory and do not behave as breeding males. All their energy is devoted to growth, which occurs rapidly.

The small males with whitish claws are dominated by the other two types of prawn and grow only slowly. Small and very agile, they sometimes take part in reproduction by slipping between a blue-clawed male and a female.

The ratio of males to females in an adult population is normally one to one; the proportions of the three morphotypes remain constant (5–10 per cent blue-clawed prawns, 10–25 per cent orange-clawed and 20–25 per cent of whitish-clawed), indicating that there is a population balance. When a dominant blue-clawed prawn disappears, due either to death or being harvested, one of the largest orange-clawed males takes its place and after moulting acquires long blue claws. The place vacated by the orange-clawed male is taken by one of the largest whitish-clawed prawns which then becomes orange-clawed.

The changes in a male, therefore, are as follows:

WHITISH CLAWS → ORANGE CLAWS → BLUE CLAWS

This restoration of the imbalance created by the disappearance of a dominant prawn, resulting in growth stimulation, is known as compensatory growth. The growth of males on a farm is governed by this phenomenon. Compensatory growth occurs when the majority of large prawns, i.e. the dominant males, are harvested.

Careful, regular harvesting of dominant males is therefore the key to further growth by the rest of the half population.

8 Farm management

8.1 *General situation*

The various species of *Macrobrachium* are farmed throughout the world using very different methods – traditional fisheries and extensive farms with family labour in southeast Asia or combined farming with carp, mullet, tilapia or catfish. *Macrobrachium rosenbergii* is managed under semi-intensive systems on specialised farms which may cover 20 or 30 hectares.

The principal aim of encouraging this type of farming in the tropics at the beginning of the 1970s was to diversify agriculture, especially in regions of monoculture, e.g. sugar cane. It provided a product with a high commercial value to be sold locally and exported. Farming is now even encouraged in areas where freshwater prawns are traditionally caught, especially since the introduction of hatcheries which permit the planned stocking of post-larvae and therefore planned harvesting and marketing too.

8.2 *Harvesting*

Various devices have been traditionally used by fishermen in southeast Asia to catch *Macrobrachium* in their natural environment. These are:

- cast nets (round weighted nets which are thrown), used in Thailand, Indonesia and the Philippines
- traps made from nets or woven bamboo, up to 200 m long, placed along the shores of estuaries, under water at high tide and trapping fish, crabs and prawns as the tide goes out; this type of fishing is commonly found throughout Asia
- traps made of strips of bamboo containing bait (fish offal, balls of clay and rice bran) put down in the evening from small boats and lifted the following morning
- **seine nets**, used in areas where there is underwater vegetation,

to catch other fish, lobsters and prawns (In the Philippines in areas where the bottom is sandy or muddy, V-shaped nets on the bows of small motorboats are pushed slowly through the water for two to three hours.)

- fishing with hooks baited with coconut (This method, which is used in Burma, catches mainly large prawns, 60–90 g.).

About 100 species of the genus *Macrobrachium* are caught throughout the world. It is difficult to give a reliable estimate of the production of prawns from both fishing and farming. It is impossible to keep accurate statistics in Asia owing partly to the numbers of sources and the wide area covered, and partly to difficulties in identifying these species, given the different local names and names given by customs authorities, which vary from one country to another. Furthermore, not all markets are included in the statistics. The principal exporting countries are Bangladesh, Thailand, Indonesia, The Philippines and Brazil (Table 4).

Table 4   The 10 principal producers of freshwater prawns caught (left column) and farmed (right column)
(FAO statistics, IFREMER Aquaculture Digest and Survey, 1989) in tonnes

Fishing		Farming	
Bangladesh	43 000	Thailand	15 000
Indonesia	13 000	Taiwan	3500
Philippines	11 000	Brazil	450
Brazil	10 000	Mexico	360
Vietnam	5000	France (Dom–Tom)	200
Thailand	4000	Dominican Republic	110
Japan	3970	Puerto Rico	90
Burma	3800	Malaysia	70
Mexico	3220	Japan	55
India	400	USA	50
Total	100 000	**Total**	20 000

8.3   Farming

Since the whole life cycle of *Macrobrachium* can now be managed in captivity, prawn farming is not dependent on natural stocks. Only a few prawns of each sex are required in a given area to start farming on a large scale. Examples of this independence from natural populations are farms which have been set up outside the species' natural habitat. In the majority of cases the first prawns came from

Hawaii from the breed known as 'Anuenue', called after the place where the Fujimura laboratory is situated in Honolulu, where the first farming methods were developed.

> ONLY A FEW PRAWNS OF EACH SEX ARE NEEDED TO START LARGE-SCALE FARMING IN A GIVEN REGION.

From its inception, freshwater prawn farming has often been considered a means of satisfying development or restructuring requirements for agricultural economies in difficulties, e.g. in regions where sugar cane is the only crop. In these cases prawn farming is introduced into a regional programme and used for diversification of small agricultural businesses. The farms, which are small, are then supplied with post-larvae from a regional hatchery. There are also large individual projects, which generally include all stages – rearing, hatching and packing – often promoted by animal feed manufacturers and public utility companies.

In French overseas territories (DOM-TOM) freshwater prawn farming, which began in the early 1980s on an appreciable scale, has been able to satisfy local market demand (Tahiti, Martinique and Guadeloupe) for a product that is highly-rated, widely known and rare. It was included in a large agricultural development programme in French Guiana as a short-term speculation for export to France. The development stage covered a period of ten years in all, with considerable activity from 1983 to 1986, when prawn farming was introduced into the Antilles and Guiana. The end of growth from 1987 on corresponded to saturation of the Antilles market and a halt to development in Guiana as a result of export problems. The solution should be found in a marketing policy implemented at the end of 1988.

9 Farming techniques

THERE ARE TWO STAGES TO PRAWN FARMING:

- the first, to obtain the post-larvae – the larvae rearing stage in a hatchery
- the second, to produce prawns of marketable size. This is farming in the strict sense of the word, i.e. rearing, which takes place in earthen ponds.

The broodstock required for each new cycle generally comes from stock in the rearing stage, from which berried females are removed.

9.1 Post-larvae production (rearing larvae): the hatchery stage

Characteristics of *Macrobrachium rosenbergii* larval development

This stage, the only one that must take place in brackish water, involves reproducing, in a controlled environment, the conditions required for the development of larvae in their natural surroundings. *Macrobrachium rosenbergii* larvae kept in fresh water die after two days, as do those kept in normal sea water. (The larvae of some *Macrobrachium* species from islands in the Tropics develop in sea water, e.g. *Macrobrachium lar* from the Pacific area.)

Morphologically, larvae develop very gradually from stage 1 – the hatching stage when they are 2 mm long, their eyes are sessile and the only complete appendages are the cephalic appendages – to stage 2, the stage preceding metamorphosis when they are 8 mm long and all appendages are fully formed. Development is slow, an average of two days for each stage, with the first post-larvae appearing between the 18th and 22nd day.

Weight increase is less uniform. For the first 12 days, weights increase by a coefficient of 2.5 (0.3 to 0.75 mg). During this period of rapid weight increase, nutritional requirements in terms of animal protein are considerable. On about the 20th day their requirements are 100 per cent of their own weight in hydrated food per day.

Owing to larval stage characteristics (a large number of stages, very gradual development and considerable nutritional requirements) there is a risk in prawn farming of prolonging the length of the cycle and so increasing the spread of larval stages, of extending the period of metamorphosis and of contaminating the water with excreta and food waste. Such risks may lead to increased mortality and a reduction in the numbers of post-larvae produced.

Hatching techniques, which have gradually been developed, vary according to the importance given to prevention of these risks. The most effective are those designed to control:

- factors determining larval development (environment and nutrition)
- the quality of the water throughout the cycle.

Example of an intensive system - The Pacific Oceanology Centre (IFREMER) system

Introduction
This system had three objectives:

- first, to make units independent of the external environment around the hatchery so that they would not be affected by changes in temperature or other environmental factors
- second, to be able to exercise continual control over the units in order to regulate the growth of stock
- third, to reduce the risk of neglecting proper daily maintenance in order to ensure that the results of successive production cycles are as near a standard as possible and to make it possible for workers with no previous training to carry out the work.

Under this system, the types of building, equipment, procedure and processes have consequently been defined and developed in relation to each other to achieve the reliability desired.

Description of a hatchery (Guyane Aquaculture SA, a subsidiary of IFREMER, Cayenne, French Guiana)
Several operations relating to the rearing of larvae take place at the hatchery (see figs. 35, 36 and 37):

- hatching
- preparation of water for the units
- feed preparation (*Artemia* nauplii [brine shrimp] and compound feeds)
- activation of the bacterial biomass for biological filtering
- holding and delivering post-larvae (Fig. 37)
- optical observation of larvae and chemical analysis of the water

- supplying the site with sea water, fresh water, air and energy (primary supply and emergency backup)
- equipment maintenance.

Each of these is a specialised operation, distinct from the others in both where and how it is carried out. This subdivision of the hatchery allows each function to be run at a technically optimal level, it simplifies supplies of water, air and power (including the emergency backup) and permits their adaptation to precise requirements and, finally, it helps sanitary conditions by isolating the different biological processes involved (spawning tanks, larval rearing, holding post-larvae, *Artemia* incubation, activating the bacterial filtering biomass).

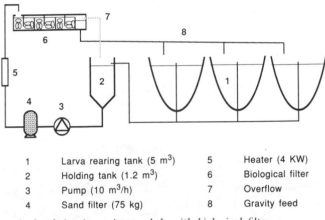

1	Larva rearing tank (5 m³)	5	Heater (4 KW)
2	Holding tank (1.2 m³)	6	Biological filter
3	Pump (10 m³/h)	7	Overflow
4	Sand filter (75 kg)	8	Gravity feed

Fig 35   *A closed-circuit rearing module with biological filter*

Fig 36   *Larva rearing area (photo: Denis Lacroix, IFREMER)*

61

Fig 37   *Holding area and delivery of post-larvae (counting using a graduated landing net) (photo: Denis Lacroix, IFREMER)*

Each operator has specific daily duties, relating to production, maintenance, monitoring and controlling batches and treatment to be given.

Work associated with production
Counting and handling larvae and post-larvae
Counting needs to be accurate, and re-checking should be carried

out by several members of staff; stock must be handled carefully.
Counting takes place:
- at the beginning of each batch: The stocking density is 100 larvae per litre. After collection in a hatching tank where they are attracted by light, larvae are counted by taking samples from a specific volume of water.
- at the end of rearing when the post-larvae are harvested. Various methods are used:
    * taking a sample in a given volume of water, or using graduated landing nets after draining the water off
    * counting while a batch is being reared can only be done accurately by sampling if larvae are uniformly distributed throughout the tank; such distribution is only possible using aeration in circular, conical bottom tanks.

Larvae have to be handled when they are moved. Mechanical stress must be avoided by the correct use of concentration devices, and physiological stress by keeping the water temperatures constant.

Preparation of water
The procedure used depends on the quality of the sea water and fresh water available on the site. The object is to have good quality water constantly available throughout the year. In order to achieve this:
- all particles in suspension must be removed by allowing them to settle and then filtering them using a sand filter of the type used in swimming pools
- water is treated with chlorine for at least 24 hours (calcium hypochlorite with 3 ppm active chlorine) to reduce the number of bacteria; it is then dechlorinated using sodium thiosulphate (7 mg/litre thiosulphate will fix 1 mg/litre free chlorine producing sodium chloride) before use.

Young larvae are very sensitive to free chlorine. A careful check is carried out to ensure that this has been removed by putting a few drops of a colouring reagent, ortho-tolidine, in a 10 ml sample of the water.

In the original system, all water in the rearing tanks was changed every day. The tank for the preparation of brackish water is in the rearing area to ensure that the temperatures of the rearing water and the new water are the same.

In the system in which biological filtering is used, the water is not changed – unless it becomes necessary for some particular reason, e.g. if the filter is not working properly – until the first post-larvae are harvested. The preparation tanks are therefore sited outside the rearing area.

Preparation and use of the biological filter

The bacteria in the nitrogen cycle, which transform ammonia excreted by larvae into nitrites and then nitrates, grow on pieces of coral in bags each holding 10 litres. The bacteria are activated by a volatile alkali (commercial ammonia at 22° or 28° Baumé: 22° B = 192 g of NH_4/l in solution) or an ammonium salt, e.g. citrate. Two different methods are used for activating bacteria.

• In the biological filter – as the larvae develop, the excretion of ammonia stimulates the development of bacteria started by ammonium citrate ten days before stocking with larvae.

• Putting increasing amounts of volatile alkali into a tank outside the larva-rearing area before the cycle commences until the oxidising capacity of the ammonia and nitrates in 24 hours is equivalent to that required during rearing. The bags of activated coral will be transferred gradually during rearing as the amount of ammonia excreted increases.

The second method is a separate operation in the hatchery which requires a specially equipped area and the extra daily task of managing the bacterial biomass. The results are, however, less variable, especially in hatcheries which operate continually throughout the year.

QUALITY OF WATER IN A HATCHERY

Allow particles to settle
  Filter
    Chlorinate, dechlorinate and check
Pay particular attention to the biological filter for removing the ammonia produced during rearing.

Food preparation

Larvae are fed on live and frozen *Artemia* nauplii and a dry or wet compound feed ('acal') based on squid and fed in the form of pellets, the size of which depends on the size of the larvae.

Artemia cysts are treated with calcium hypochlorite before incubation in order to sterilise the outer surface and facilitate hatching. Incubation takes place in a warm environment in the light. Most (60 per cent) of the nauplii are recovered after 24 hours; the remainder (15 per cent) are recovered in 42 hours. The nauplii and cysts are separated by being drawn off gradually and washed through a 200 micron mesh sieve, which allows the nauplii to pass through.

Live nauplii are given twice a day at 8 a.m. and 1 p.m. Frozen

Fig 38 *A biological filter: putting in the bags of activated substrate (photo: Denis Lacroix, IFREMER)*

nauplii are given regularly at 7 a.m. or as a standby when it has not been possible to collect sufficient fresh nauplii for the day.

The quantity of nauplii required per day is calculated from a feed table improved on as the technique was developed. The number of cysts to be incubated is deduced from the nauplii requirements given in the table and from the hatching rate of cysts, checked two or three times during the rearing cycle by taking a sample from a known volume of water after ad hoc dilution of the sample.

The compound algae feed is used dry (as it is purchased), or fresh. In this case it is produced daily at the hatchery.

The particles used must be of the correct size, which is increased as the larvae grow. This feed is given at 10 a.m. and 4 p.m.

Maintenance work on units

- Maintenance work during rearing or when the tanks are empty is facilitated by the shape of the tanks, which are circular with conical bottoms or in the form of deep rectangular baths parabolic in section, and by the material used in their construction (fibreglass-reinforced polyester resin). The following equipment has been specially designed for the use and maintenance of the tanks:
  * a central bayonet-fitting overflow one third of the way from the top
  * a central filter with removable sleeves (four sleeves with mesh from 0.189 to 0.7 mm are provided for each tank)
  * air intakes located at specific positions in the tank to mix the water uniformly
  * a foam-rubber brush to clean algal or bacterial growth from the underwater part of the tank wall
  * a siphon to remove food waste from the centre of the tank bottom after stirring the water with a special paddle
  * a viewing-glass or magnifying glass to observe the larvae under water and the post-larvae on the wall
  * a sponge to remove dead larvae adhering to the edge of the tank under water.

  This equipment is cleaned after use with chlorinated water in a tank adjacent to the rearing tanks, then allowed to dry.

- Solid waste in suspension (food waste, *Artemia* cysts, moulted shells, faeces) is removed from the tanks when the water is exchanged, which in the original system takes place once a day in the evening. In the closed circuit system, waste is continually being removed through the biological filter. The size of the central filter sleeve mesh depends on the size of the larvae.

  In the closed circuit system most of the waste removed from the tank is held in the sand filter, which is cleaned twice a day at 7 a.m. and 1 p.m. by blowing air onto the opposite side of the filter.

  Some of the waste is also deposited in the closed circuit or recycling piping or in the biological filter in the form of foam on the wall above the water from the effect of aeration, or on the bacterial substrate, which may become choked. For this reason, the pipework, closed circuit holding tank and inside of the biological filter are cleaned every other day from the 15th day.

- In addition to regular maintenance, elementary sanitary precautions are taken to reduce the risk of infection by pathogenic bacteria. These bacteria do not come from outside the hatchery but appear among bacteria which grow during rearing in the warm, damp atmosphere of the hatchery. They adapt to the larvae and may become virulent, especially for young larvae. Two types of precaution are taken to reduce this risk:
  * between each batch the hatchery is emptied and all equipment thoroughly cleaned using chlorine and an antibacterial product based on quaternary ammonia; all pipework etc. is dismantled and allowed to dry
  * while a batch is being reared, each tank must retain its own equipment and no maintenance or other equipment is ever transferred to another tank at the hatchery.

SANITARY PRECAUTIONS – AN ABSOLUTE NECESSITY

Between each batch everything must be:
- cleaned
- dismantled
- dried.

During rearing make certain that the equipment for a tank is used for that tank only. Never use a set of equipment for another tank!

Monitoring and controlling batches

This involves environmental factors, water analysis and observation of the larvae.

Environmental factors

In addition to salinity, the factors directly affecting larval development are temperature, which determines the time spent at different stages, and light, which influences larval activity, principally feeding.

Hatcheries are designed so that these two factors may be easily controlled. They are in a closed space, which reduces the effect of external temperature. There are large windows to provide plenty of light from the side at tank level; translucent roofing is used to provide a balance of light inside.

The temperature is maintained at the optimum level (29–31°C) by a heater in the closed circuit; it can be controlled either automatically by a thermostat or manually. When on wet days there is insufficient light, 400 W spotlights above the tanks are switched on.

The temperature in the tanks is checked at 7 a.m. and 4 p.m. When preparing water for rearing, salinity is checked by a refractometer or a salinometer. Salinity is kept at 1.2 per cent throughout the rearing period; bacterial flora are also active in water of 1.2 per cent salinity. Post-larvae are held at 0.4 per cent and delivered at 0.2 per cent. Water is analysed principally for the following:

- to check ammonia and nitrite levels in batches of larvae and in the bacterial biomass activating tank for the biological filter; the colorimetric method using a kit and spectrophotometer is employed
- to check chlorine (ortho-tolidine) levels in the rearing water preparation tanks.

The maximum accepted concentrations are:

- ammonia: 1 mg/l $N–NH_3/NH^{4+}$, or 1.3 mg/l NH_3 NH^{4+}
- nitrites: 0.3 mg/l $N–NO_2$ or 0.9 mg NO_2
- chlorine: 0.1 mg/l free chlorine.

Daily observation

This is an essential part of management since it enables the progress of the batches to be forecast from the situation ascertained from measurements and analyses.

Direct observation is facilitated in this system since there is only a small volume of water, which is clear. When aeration is stopped, larval behaviour can be observed and food remains and dead larvae seen. Healthy larvae come to the surface where they congregate in large masses; they are well pigmented and very active, catching *Artemia* on the surface or taking alginated particles. If they attempt to attack each other, this means either that there is insufficient food (and they are fighting for it) or that some larvae are weaker than others owing to an outbreak of bacterial disease or external parasites, or even moulting larvae being poisoned by a high concentration of ammonia or nitrites.

A microscope (100, 250 and 400 magnification) may be used to confirm direct observation and identify the cause of abnormal behaviour.

There are different types of bacteria:

- **chitinolytic bacteria**, which are responsible for necrosis (black patches surrounded by rod-shaped bacteria) on the youngest appendages
- filamentous bacteria (*Leucothrix*) growing on parts of the body where there are currents of water
- bacteria in the digestive tract responsible for the disease 'black

spot' (granular appearance of stomach and empty digestive tract). External parasites are mostly ciliates (*Epistylis* or others) or moulds which may completely cover the body surface, giving it a woolly appearance. If there are hydroids on the tank wall, the **integuments** of the larvae may be affected by nematocysts, resulting in death if the infestation is serious.

Problems associated with water quality are deformation of the cephalic appendages (at the base of the antennae and antennules) in the form of 'handlebars' – the result of a failed moult; affected larvae go to the bottom of the tank and very soon die.

Microscopic observations are made on either several larvae taken from the tank or waste recovered during the daily siphoning of the tank (which is carried out at 1 p.m.).

Digestive activity may be assessed by using a binocular magnifying glass (16 and 40 magnification) to determine the stage of larval development and stomach fullness index.

A sample of 80 larvae per tank is examined every day to establish the average larval development stage (Table 5). It is essential to know and monitor this indicator, known as the larval stage index (LSI), which is the weighted average of the stages examined, since it enables growth to be checked daily to ascertain whether it is normal or retarded. The indicator is entered on a chart at the hatchery which shows the LSIs of all tanks. The person responsible for the hatchery can therefore have an overall view of the rearing in progress.

The LSI is calculated every day at 8 a.m. by taking a sample from each tank to the laboratory. If it indicates retarded development, the cause must be identified.

Table 5 Criteria for recognising larval stages

Stages	Criteria
1	**Sessile** eyes
2	Stalked eyes
3	Uropods appear
4	Development of the 5th pereopod
5	Development of the 4th pereopod
6	Pleopod buds appear
7	3rd segment of antennal flagellum appears, biramous pleopods
8	Setae appear on the pleopods
9	Internal appendage appears on pleopods' endopodite
10	Teeth appear on upper surface of the rostrum
11	Teeth appear on lower surface of the rostrum

The stomach fullness index (IR) is calculated twice a day at 9.30 a.m. and 4 p.m. from 50 larvae after feeding, i.e. when the stomachs are full. An index of 100 signifies a full stomach; 75 signifies 3/4 full; 50 signifies half full. The weighted average of individual indexes gives the average IR. An average index of under 75 and no signs of food remains is an indicator of lack of food. If food remains are observed, the IR then indicates that there is a disease problem.

Recording information

The following measurements, analyses, observations and unusual occurrences are entered every day in notebooks and record charts.
- a chart for each tank (date, temperature, LSI, food – type and amount, IR, maintenance)
- a daily chart for *Artemia* preparation and hatching rates entered in a notebook
- a fresh compound feed preparation chart
- a notebook for products observed when siphoning a tank
- a notebook for harvesting, holding and delivery of post-larvae
- a notebook for monitoring the functioning of the biological filters and transfer of the active substrate.

It is essential to record all this information in order to check the work of the operators, build up a record for the hatchery and enable the system to be improved.

Treatment of batches

Batches must be subjected to careful regular inspection in order to identify problems as soon as they appear so that appropriate action may be taken. Lack of inspection and monitoring may result in the sudden loss of whole tanks since carelessness of this nature is almost always associated with inefficient maintenance.

There are two basic operations:
- exchanging the water
- treatment with antibiotics.

In the recirculating system, water should be changed when the biological filter is not working properly and does not restrict concentrations of ammonia and nitrites. When the NO_2 concentration is above 1 mg/l, the water has undergone a partial change.

All water should be exchanged when, as well as containing high concentrations of ammonia and nitrites, it is dirty and the sand filter is unable to keep it clean.

Treatment with antibiotics is necessary when larvae are infected by bacteria or parasites or when there are signs of malformation. Several antibiotics have been tried – penicillin, tetracycline, aureomycin and chloramphenicol.

Chloramphenicol is the most widely used at present since it has a very wide antibacterial spectrum. It acts directly on the bacteria commonly found on farms. In the case of external parasites and physiological stress, it acts as a factor in restoring larvae to health, either through its own properties, or by controlling bacteria which attack weak larvae.

Decreasing doses of chloramphenicol are given for three consecutive days, starting with 30 mg/m^3 the first day, 20 g/m^3 the second day and finally 10 g/m^3 the third day. Treatment, which is more effective in clean than dirty water, is normally carried out after the water has been exchanged, chloramphenicol being put into clean water while the tank is being filled. It can be used while the circuit is closed and the biological filter is functioning since chloramphenicol does not act on the bacteria in the nitrogen cycle.

Note: Use of chloramphenicol for aquacultural purposes is not permitted in North America or Europe, and its use in the tropics should be minimised, since it is one of the few drugs that is effective against human bacterial diseases such as cholera.

Delivery of post-larvae

After metamorphosis, post-larvae are kept in the hatchery for four days before being sent to farms.

They are delivered in plastic bags half full of water with a very low salt content (0.2 per cent). The bags are put inside plastic containers or cartons for protection; 50 litre bags with 20 litres of water may contain 8000 post-larvae. The top half of the bag is filled with oxygen under very low pressure and sealed using two rubber bands. When sending post-larvae by air, bags are only partially inflated, in order to avoid the risk of bursting from partial depressurisation, and the density of post-larvae is reduced to 200/l. Using this method excellent survival rates are obtained after 48 hours' transport.

DELIVERY

- Open a 50-litre plastic bag.
- Fill with 20 litres of water.
- Put in 8000 freshwater prawn post-larvae.
- Inflate with oxygen, but not excessively.
- Seal.
- Put the bag in a carton or box.
- Send or transport.

9.2 Pond rearing

The principle

Freshwater prawns are reared in earthen ponds until they are ready for sale. This is a semi-intensive method. Some factors are controlled by the farmer, e.g. the number of prawns in a pond, the amount of compound feed, control of predators and competitors, water exchanging, drain harvesting. However, he has no control over physio-chemical environmental parameters such as soil and water quality, sunlight, rainfall, temperature and wind, which depend on the natural environment round the pond and the local climate.

Under these conditions the maximum biomass which may be obtained at any given time is 100–200 g prawns per square metre and the total yield of a unit is between 2 and 3 tonnes/hectare per year, with classes ranging from 10–20 to 40–50 prawns per kilogram, the majority being in the 20–30 and 30–40 prawns per kilogram classes.

Different ways of managing the population (farming schedules)

Managing the population takes into consideration:
- the natural organisation into hierarchical groups
- the very uneven growth of individuals within a batch and, in the case of males, the phenomenon of compensatory growth (section 7.6).

Various operations are necessary during the life of a crop; these are generally of the following two types:
- the regular culling of dominant individuals, harvesting them when they are of marketable size; their places in the hierarchy are taken up by smaller prawns which then gain weight rapidly
- sorting the prawns into uniform batches; the small prawns then form a normal population with the dominant animals growing rapidly.

The principal methods of management are based on these two operations.

The continuous system

This, the oldest method, developed by Fujimura at Hawaii, is based on continuous stocking with post-larvae at regular intervals and on cull harvesting large prawns when they are of marketable size. The pond may be used continuously for four or five years.

This originally simple system, which has undergone improvements with respect to timing of stocking and methods of monitoring and controlling crops, was devised by the IFREMER team working in the Antilles and Guiana in 1982. The system encouraged the development of farms in these regions.

Plate A   Louisiana red swamp crayfish

Plate B   Red swamp crayfish caught in Sarcelles, France

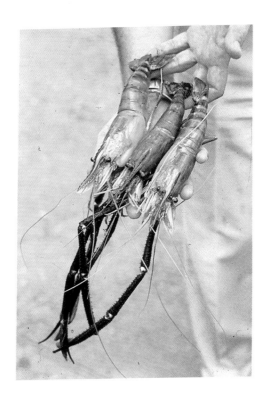

Plate C Macrobrachium, the giant freshwater prawn or crayfish
(photo: Denis Lacroix, IFREMER)

Plate D   Paenaeus, the penaeid prawn

Plate E   Berried (egg-carrying) females at the beginning (yellow eggs) and
at the end (grey eggs) of the incubation stage (photo: Denis Lacroix,
IFREMER)

Plate F Three male morphoptypes and a female from a population of
freshwater prawns (photo: Denis Lacroix, IFREMER)

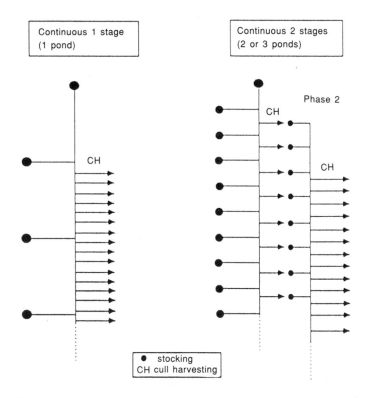

Fig 39 *Principle of the continuous management method – in one stage and two stages*

A variation is used on a large scale at the Sabana Grande farm in Puerto Rico. This farm employs the continuous system in two stages, the second stage being one of regularly stocking with prawns pre-reared to an average of 7–10 g and selected during the first rearing stage.

The batch (discontinuous) system

In its simplest form this involves rearing a batch of post-larvae stocked only once, to marketable size, first cull harvesting then harvesting all the animals by draining the pond, which is then refilled with water for another batch. A proportion, which depends on age and stocking rate, will not have reached marketable size when draining takes place. These prawns are generally put into another pond to complete rearing.

There are many variations of the batch method. The most elaborate, and therefore the most difficult to manage, consists of regularly

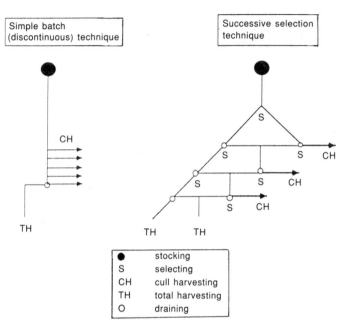

Fig 40   *Principle of batch (discontinuous) management and management by uniform batches through successive selection*

dividing the crop into uniform batches, sorting the animals to allow them all to grow to marketable size more quickly.

Pre-rearing (the nursery stage)
These different systems may all include an initial stage, the pre-rearing or nursery stage, which corresponds to the start of growth of prawns and transition from the post-larval to the juvenile stage. Pre-rearing has several advantages for rearing and production:

- Since post-larvae are very small (between 10 and 20 mg), the stocking density may be very high (up to $250/m^2$). The rearing area is consequently better occupied than in the case of direct stocking of a rearing pond, while the area kept for pre-rearing is very productive (in two months the average weight reaches 0.5 g, which represents a biomass of $125 \ g/m^2$ per 250 juveniles; five crops per year produce 6.25 tonnes of biomass per hectare).
- Since nursery ponds are small, they can be managed better and there will be better control over both the physical and chemical parameters of the rearing environment and the feed, the quality, form, size and distribution of which must be suitable. This

type of monitoring results in a survival rate of up to two months better than when rearing pools are stocked directly.

- At the end of the pre-rearing period prawns are stronger and better acclimatised to their environment than post-larvae and there will be very little risk of mortality when they are transferred to the rearing ponds, thus enabling the producer to rely more on his crop.

Choice of management method

Although in theory there are methods of management which enable a population with this degree of hierarchy to be exploited more fully and rationally, in practice the method used depends on a number of factors which make one method more effective than another in any given situation.

The following are the principal factors to be taken into consideration:

- local climate, especially temperature variations throughout the year: if there is a cold season (temperature below 22°C for several months), discontinuous batch rearing should be used (South Carolina, Israel, La Réunion)
- the market: if the market requires large prawns (10–20 and 20–30 per kilogram), the continuous system is more suitable
- resources available: if there is little equipment or technical know-how, e.g. where prawn farming is introduced to smallholdings in the tropics for the purposes of diversification, the continuous system should be recommended.

Generally speaking:

- The continuous method only permits partial exploitation of the stock since the number of prawns sold is at best only 40 per cent of larvae stocked. It is also difficult to check feeding, and food conversion ratios (FCRs) are generally high (FCR ~ 4 : 1) for the proportion of prawns harvested.
- The discontinuous method enables the numbers of stock to be checked accurately at short intervals, so giving the farmer a more accurate picture of how the stock is shaping up. The food conversion rate is generally much lower (between 2.5 and 3).

These two systems both depend on the following:

- a pond complying with specific standards
- management of the farm environment – which affects the daily environment of the stock and their food of natural origin
- monitoring the stock and controlling its growth and mortality
- feeding
- harvesting prawns of marketable size and primary processing on the farm.

The rearing pond

The site

The following criteria must be considered when choosing a pond site:

- water resources – availability throughout the year, allowing for a ten per cent daily renewal rate of the water in all ponds
- topography (slightly sloping to keep terracing to a minimum) and nature of the soil (impervious)
- access (accessibility in all seasons) and feasibility (taking electricity to the site).

Fig 41 *A commercial farm (38 hectares) in French Guiana (photo: Denis Lacroix, IFREMER)*

Ponds

Since ponds are built to last a long time (depreciation over 15 to 20 years), it is important to comply with certain principles, especially soil compactness and the slope of the bunds. They must comply exactly with the following standards so that the rearing system can be adhered to:

- They must be rectangular (length to breadth ratio of 2 : 3.5); a maximum width of about 40 m to ensure effective harvesting and to enable the food to be distributed over the whole surface; the average area should be 0.5 hectares.
- The bottom should be smooth, hard, compacted and sloping gently towards the outlet. The minimum accepted depth is 0.7 m and maximum 1.4 m. Several problems can arise if these depths are not respected. Aquatic plants will grow where the water is shallow; where it is deep, harvesting will be impossible without partial drainage and a risk of stratification.
- Bunds must be well compacted and slope gently (1 : 3), otherwise they will collapse. They must be covered with grass to protect them from being eroded by rain. They must be at least 3 m wide to permit work to be carried on from them.

Water supply

- Water is supplied by gravity from a collection point in a stream above the ponds or by pumping from a watercourse or an underground source.
- For small farms water is brought in through PVC piping underground or through channels. If pumped water contains much sediment, this must be allowed to settle before it enters the pond. This requires special devices to be installed above the supply system. Channels allow water to clarify and must be cleaned out regularly.
- Water coming into the pond must be controlled by shut-off mechanisms (valves or sluices). These are installed at the top end of the pond above the level of the water and must be fitted with a filter in the form of a bag with a 0.5 mm mesh to prevent predator fish or competitors from entering the pond. The filter must be cleaned regularly outside the pond area. The flow can be checked by using a container of a known volume and a chronometer.
- Several different devices are used to drain the water from the pond, the oldest being the monk (made of concrete with wooden boards); the easiest to use is a concrete pit fitted with a two-way pipe, which allows water to be removed from both the bottom and the top. Outside the pond there may be a harvest sump to facilitate harvesting the prawns after draining.

Management of the rearing environment

Description

Several days after a pond is filled, a complex aquatic environment appears as a result of biological activity. This is a **eutropic** environment which is regularly supplied with organic matter from the food fed to the prawns and from **endogenous** waste; only a small proportion of it (an average of ten per cent per day) is renewed.

The environment 'digests' this organic matter by recycling it in different ways, the most important of which takes place at the bottom of the pond where all organic waste collects. The waste is broken down by successive **decomposing agents** until it forms mineral salts which enrich the zone of water in which the first stage of a normal trophic chain, the phytoplankton, develops.

This normal process:

- provides the prawns with the oxygen they need for respiration, through the phytoplankton which, like any vegetable cells, produce oxygen during the day by photosynthesis (this is the principal natural source of oxygen in the pool)
- provides the prawns with part of their food from the trophic chains, especially from the fraction at the bottom of the pool; this contribution is particularly important for the young stages
- recycles the waste, preventing concentrations from rapidly becoming lethal.

The process could become abnormal if, for example, the balance between the supply of organic matter and its recycling were broken. The fragile stage of the environment is the phytoplankton which are the first to react to this **dystrophic process**. After a period of intense development, when the water becomes very green, the phytoplankton go to the bottom overnight, die and settle out on the bottom, the water then becoming transparent. The oxygen deficiency also affects the prawns, large numbers of which may die.

It therefore appears that management of the rearing environment is essential if the farm is always to be profitable. Since there is a very large volume of water in a pond (an average of 5000 m³) and the environment at any given time is the result of a very gradual chain of different reactions (biological, chemical or physical), this environment must be managed effectively to prevent a dystrophic change rather than trying to regenerate an already degraded environment.

The farmer takes action to set up and manage the environment in order to ensure that it remains balanced, monitoring and controlling it by regularly measuring the various physical and chemical indicators relevant to its operation.

Establishment and maintenance

The quality and functioning of the rearing environment depends to a great extent on the natural environment of the ponds (mineral composition of the water and soil; abundance and diversity of the strains of plankton and other vegetable and animal matter in the water entering the pools; local climate – sunshine, rainfall, winds and temperature).

Before and during the filling of the pond the farmer must take steps to correct certain mineral and biological deficiencies and, during the rearing period, to control the growth of the phytoplankton, which is influenced by local atmospheric conditions.

Mineral deficiencies involve calcium and, to a lesser extent, magnesium, which play an important part in the biochemistry of the environment at all levels of the trophic chain. They are essential for prawns, especially calcium for hardening the carapace. Before filling the pond, the farmer must supply the necessary calcium, generally as fine calcium carbonate granules, the most effective form; between one and three tonnes are normally added per hectare per year. It is also added during growth by sprinkling it on the water.

Biological deficiencies may be corrected before filling by providing vegetable waste, e.g. rice straw activated by poultry manure at the rate of one to three tonnes per hectare per year on a semi-intensive unit.

The farmer can accelerate growth of the phytoplankton when the pond is being filled by inoculation with algal cells from a nearby pond already in use and an NPK chemical fertiliser. The floating bottle technique, which allows the fertiliser to be released slowly, is recommended.

During rearing the farmer will have to take steps to limit rather than encourage phytoplankton growth. By regularly changing the water, growth may be controlled gradually; by changing large amounts it may be controlled quickly. In order to avoid using chemicals, which may have too sudden an effect, with repercussions that will affect the prawns, the water may be made opaque by using a pump to stir up the mud on the bottom. This will have the effect of stopping reproduction of the algae by reducing the amount of light penetrating the surface water. Products for controlling the quality of the rearing environment and its development should be used carefully and gradually to enable the farmer to see their effects. Sudden treatment using large amounts of any substance must be avoided.

Environment indicators

These are temperature, pH, dissolved oxygen, water hardness, alkalinity and turbidity.

These indicators are used primarily to estimate the quality of the rearing environment. If at any time there is insufficient dissolved oxygen in the water, particularly in the water at the bottom, no action the farmer can take, apart from correcting this rapidly, will have any effect and the prawns will die. The indicators are also used to estimate the rearing environment's development, which must always safeguard against lack of oxygen.

Each indicator must be noted carefully at precise intervals. Measurements must be taken at the same time, in the same place and with identical devices, which must be calibrated regularly.

Temperature
This affects:
- growth rate, since prawns are unable to regulate their body temperatures (the optimum temperature is 28–30°C)
- the maximum amount of dissolved oxygen in the water (9.2 mg oxygen per litre at 20°C, 8.4 mg per litre at 25°C and 7.7 mg per litre at 30°C).

Temperature may be used as an accurate indicator of stratification of the water mass in a pond. The farmer must know the daily and annual temperature fluctuations in the ponds. This is basic information which is measured in the morning and evening on the surface, at the bottom and at the water intake.

pH
This is the H^+ ion content – i.e. acidity – of the water. Its value and variations are directly linked with the biological activity in a pond. It increases by day as a result of oxygen produced by phytoplankton photosynthesis and it decreases at night through generation of carbon dioxide from respiration of all living organisms in the pond. pH plays an important role in chemical reactions which take place in the pond and in the body processes of prawns (in ion exchanges across cell membranes).

The optimum pH for prawns is between 7 and 8.5. A pH of over 9 is lethal for post-larvae. It is the duration of exposure to extremes – low (5.0) and high (over 9.5) – and rapid changes which cause mortality, rather than extreme values on their own. The speed of change depends on the buffering capacity of the water, resulting from its carbon ion (CO^{3-}) and bicarbonate (HCO^{3-}) content. In water with total hardness of 60 mg/l of $CaCO_3$ equivalent, pH will vary more slowly than in water with 20 mg/l.

On the other hand, the more the pH increases, the more ammonia, which is excreted by prawns, is in the form of toxic NH_3:

- at 30°C at pH7 the ammonia is broken down into 0.7% NH_3 + 99.3% NH^{4+}
- at pH9 ammonia is broken down into 40% NH_3 + 60% H^{4+}

pH is measured either by a colorimetric pH meter (Hach, Cifec) or by an electronic pH meter.

In practice the colorimetric pH meter is often preferred in spite of being less accurate (by one fifth). In hot humid climates electronic pH meters lose their accuracy very quickly and have to be recalibrated frequently.

pH must be measured regularly, in the morning at 7 a.m. and in the evening at 5 p.m.

Dissolved oxygen

This is the most important parameter to be checked. It must be measured at the bottom where the prawns live. In uniform environments the oxygen content in the surface layers of water and at the bottom are similar and change in parallel during the day, while in stratified ponds these values may be very different and change independently.

At 2 mg/l oxygen the balance of nutrition required can no longer be maintained; the prawns endeavour to get away from the bottom and go up to the edge of the pond, their muscles become opaque and they die. The concentration required for normal growth is between 5 and 7 mg/litre.

It is normally towards the end of the night, at about 4 o'clock in the morning, when prawns leave the bottom because of oxygen deficiency. The reserves built up during the previous day by phytoplankton photosynthesis are insufficient to satisfy the demand for oxygen of the living creatures in the pond (from the prawns to bacteria) and the chemical demand for mineral oxides.

The farmer may then have to take action, mixing and aerating the rearing environment by mechanical means. Methods suitable for prawns reared under these conditions are:
- using a microturbine and air injection, by a venturi effect (AIRE-02 aerator)
- using paddles to stir up the surface of the water (a paddle-wheel aerator).

These mixers/aerators may be permanently installed on farms where high yields are required, i.e. where large biomasses are required during any stage of production. They can be used in emergencies and only for preventing accidents. Emergency aerators are generally driven by a tractor power take-off.

Oxygen content is generally measured in situ using an electronic oxygen meter with a sensor. Some of these instruments are very

Fig 42   *AIRE 02 microturbine mixer/aerator (photo: Denis Lacroix, IFREMER)*

Fig 43   *Paddle-mixer/aerator used in an emergency (photo: Denis Lacroix, IFREMER)*

robust and reliable and remain accurate, unlike pH meters. The oxygen sensor is generally linked to a temperature sensor, thus enabling both parameters to be measured at the same time.

A measurement taken in the morning at 7 a.m. enables the values reached at the end of the night to be estimated. A measurement taken in the evening at 5 p.m. enables the values to be forecast. If there is any risk of deficiency, the farmer can take action.

Hardness

This indicates the calcium and magnesium concentration and is measured by a colorimetric method. Calcium is required for growth and to harden the carapace. The minimum amount required for rearing is 20 mg/l $CaCO_3$ equivalent. If the water is not hard enough, the farmer must provide extra calcium and magnesium before filling the pond and then by stages during the course of rearing.

Alkalinity

This is the concentration of carbonates and bicarbonates and is also measured using a colorimeter. The amount of bicarbonates and carbonates determines the number of H^+ ions which could be released (during the day) or fixed (during the night).

Alkalinity must be at least the equivalent of 20 mg/l $CaCO_3$. Below this buffer, capacity is negligible. Alkalinity is corrected by providing calcium carbonate and this is therefore included in the overall process of control.

Turbidity

The origin of turbidity may be:

- biological – caused by single-celled algae in suspension in the water, which may exceed a density of 100 000 cells per millilitre
- soil – caused by mineral particles in suspension, generally in a wet period when they are brought into the pool during pumping or more often down erosion channels in badly protected bunds.

Where there is little soil turbidity, biological turbidity is measured using a **Secchi disc**, which gives an indication of phytoplankton growth. This growth increases on sunny days as the density of algal cells increases. By taking measurements daily the farmer will learn to relate Secchi disc readings with the pH and oxygen readings taken at the same time every day so that he can calibrate the disc for the conditions on his farm. Readings must be between 20 and 50 cm.

By checking all these parameters regularly, the farmer will get to know the environment, be able to forecast changes and to act at the right time to maintain a balance favourable to the survival and growth of his stock.

Stock management

Whichever rearing system is used, continuous or discontinuous, the farmer must know precisely the numbers of prawns, their average weight and the proportions of the different types in each pool for the following reasons:

- numbers – to know whether there have been any abnormal losses

since the pond was stocked with a known number of post-larvae
- average weight – to monitor growth
- proportions of different types – for harvesting management.

The biomass may be calculated from the number and average weight of prawns to establish the right amount of food to be provided. The farmer will use several techniques at different stages of rearing, when stocking with post-larvae, during rearing and when harvesting in order to obtain these indicators. When handling the animals, he can examine them to check their condition, i.e. colour, whether any appendages have been damaged, the presence of necrosis on the carapace, etc.

Checking numbers

The numbers of post-larvae stocked at the commencement of rearing will be known. Considerable mortality can occur on stocking if environmental conditions are unfavourable or if there are predatory fish in the pond. These must be eliminated before stocking with post-larvae by using a **rotenone**-based piscicide (at 0.10–0.24 ppm pure rotenone).

The principal cause of heavy losses of post-larvae is high pH, which must be below 9. The risk of mortality is considerably less if stocking takes place in the evening rather than at the beginning or middle of the morning when the pH is higher.

Stocking is controlled by using a monitoring cage (a cube-shaped

Fig 44   *Checking a monitor cage (photo: Denis Lacroix, IFREMER)*

Fig 45   *Sampling using a special net (photo: Denis Lacroix, IFREMER)*

cage with walls of mosquito netting with mesh 1 mm wide × 0.5 mm long holding 50 post-larvae let down to the bottom of the pool, using two cages per pool). Counting, which is carried out after 24 and 48 hours, only gives an indication of survival, not an accurate estimate.

Since it is more difficult to estimate numbers during rearing, statistical methods have to be used.

WHEN SHOULD STOCKING TAKE PLACE?

In the evening rather than morning

Calculation of average weight

This is done by sampling the population by catching a small number of giant freshwater prawns using a small mesh net (4–6 mm). The average size of this net is 30 × 3 m.

Netting is done from the bund; one end of the net is held fast while the other end describes a large semi-circle through the water. The prawns caught in the net bag are put into a floating cage for inspection, measuring, weighing, sorting and marking.

Since prawns are not distributed uniformly in a pond – the smaller animals tend to be found near the water intake and the largest in the deep parts – netting must be carried out several times and in different parts of the pond in order to obtain a representative sample of the population.

The freshwater prawns caught are weighed together in a cage of a known weight, then counted (Fig. 46). The average weight of an individual is obtained by dividing the total weight by the number of prawns. If a large number of prawns have to be weighed and counted, e.g. when a pond is drained, only the total weight can be used and the average weight calculated from samples taken regularly while the prawns are being harvested.

The average weight is calculated once a month and recorded on a graph showing the growth of the population (Fig. 47). This is compared with other curves to check if rearing is progressing satis-

Fig 46   *Sample of prawns in the bag of a special net used for sampling (photo: Denis Lacroix, IFREMER)*

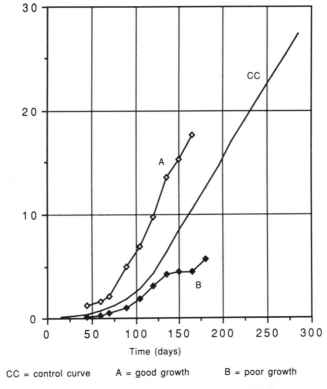

Average weight (g)

CC = control curve   A = good growth   B = poor growth

Fig 47   *Growth curves obtained by calculating average weights*

factorily. A curve with an abnormally slow rise may be the result of using an inferior feed or of not feeding enough, unfavourable environmental parameters or aggressiveness among the prawns preventing growth.

Feeding
Giant freshwater prawns are fed regularly with a compound feed but they also feed on the very varied natural food which develops in the pond, especially on the debris which accumulates in it. Under certain conditions the food from natural resources may be very important, but it is very difficult to quantify this accurately.

The compound feed must be made up to satisfy the known requirements of prawns in terms of both quality and quantity. Some of the quality requirements are known and many feeds are made up according to these requirements.

Table 6   Nutritional requirements of the freshwater prawn

Nutrients	% of dry weight
Protein	25–30
Lipids	4–6
Minerals (Ca, P)	12–16
Fibre	10
Vitamins A, D3, E, C and B6	0.5

Table 7   Example of the composition of a prawn food used in French Guiana

Composition	% of dry weight
Broken rice	9
Rice bran	15
Wheatings	10.2
Palm kernel cake	10
Soya bean cake	25
Fish meal	7.5
Meat meal	5
CPSP soluble fish protein concentrate	5
Premix (vitamins + minerals)	5
Calcium carbonate	7.5
Binding agent	0.8

Compound food

This is given in the form of pellets. The quality of the food depends on its manufacture as well as its constituents and formulation. All meal must be finely ground and particle size must be uniform to ensure that there are no fracture areas in the pellets. When pellets are manufactured by dry pressing using steam, it is essential to use a binding agent to ensure that they remain whole for at least two hours after feeding. This allows the prawns, which are slow feeders, to consume most of the constituents.

Feeding

The quality to be given depends on the age of the prawns and the temperature. Table 8 shows the proportions used for water temperatures of 28–30°C.

Table 8 Calculation of required quantity according to age of the population

Age (months)	1	2	3	4	5	6	etc.
% of the biomass	8	6	4	3	2	2	2

On a continuous system the ration will be 25 to 30 kg/ha per day for a stabilised population.

Prawns are generally fed once a day only, at the end of the afternoon, since adults are particularly active at night. Pellets must be distributed uniformly over the surface of the pond so that they will be accessible to all individuals and so limit competition. They are distributed either by hand or mechanically using a spinning blade or pneumatic distributor.

Controlling food consumption
It is difficult to check food consumption so as to adjust the amounts to be given regularly (the proportions given must be considered as bases for calculation), especially if the pellets break up quickly in water. Different methods used are: troughs, pellets scattered on the surface, underwater observation (when it is not too cloudy), scraping the bottom with a fine mesh net. Some specialists have developed statistical methods based on observing surface injuries on the prawns (antennae or appendages broken off and other injuries). The amount of feed given is increased when the proportion of injured animals increases.

Whatever method is used by the stockman, it is important for food consumption to be controlled. Food cost is a very large item in the cost of producing prawns and so gauging food requirements accurately can encourage important savings.

> The conversion rate indicates the amount of food given in order to produce 1 kg of prawns of marketable size. Experience has shown that farmers always tend to feed too much, with the result that food – i.e. money – is wasted and the rearing environment deteriorates rapidly.

Under the discontinuous system, precise monitoring of the population and of food consumption can lead to conversion ratios (FCR values) of 2.5. Under the continuous system they may exceed 4.

Storage

Certain precautions must be taken when storing food on the farm to avoid rapid deterioration, especially of vitamins. The food store must be well ventilated or air-conditioned to protect the food from heat and humidity. In order to facilitate air circulation and avoid mould, bags should be on pallets, not stacked on the ground.

Food is the production factor which has a significant effect on productivity. Improved productivity will be obtained not only by improving feed quality (compound feed and the stimulated natural productivity of the pond) but also by adapting the feeding method to take better account of timing and of behavioural requirements.

Harvesting

This is generally carried out by culling. Even where harvesting is completed by draining the pond, this is preceded by culling, so as to reduce the numbers to be handled and sorted.

- Cull harvesting is carried out using a net with a mesh suitable for the size of prawns to be harvested. A mesh 25 mm wide may be used for prawns weighing 40 g and a 20 mm mesh for prawns weighing 25 g. Smaller mesh nets are used when the prawns are sorted; a 14 mm mesh is used for 9 g prawns.

- A harvest net will be at least twice the width of the pool. It must be about 80 m long in order to harvest a pool 40 m wide effectively. It will have an effective depth (with square mesh) of 2.5 to 3 m. It is generally a set net and may have a bag 2 m deep either half way between the long sides or in the first third. The bag is either fixed or held on with a zip fastener so that it can be removed after harvesting to take out the prawns. The net may then be used immediately in another pool using another bag.

  The net is well weighted at 200 to 300 g per running metre. This weight enables the bottom of the pool to be swept to ensure that all the prawns go into or pass through the net. In muddy ponds it is more difficult to pull a weighted net since the weights sink into the mud. One method of overcoming this involves using lighter weights (100–150 g per metre) and a thick rope fastened along the bottom of the net; the rope then slides over the mud.

  The top of the net must be on the surface (5–6 floats per metre) so that the prawns cannot get over the top.

- Four to six people are required for harvesting. The net is pulled along the length of the pond in a sweep along the bunds. Care must be taken to ensure that the net does not come off the

Fig 48   *Cull harvesting (photo: Denis Lacroix, IFREMER)*

bottom. When the whole pond has been trawled, the bag is closed near the water intake in order to wash the prawns and provide them with the oxygen they require. A tractor may be used to pull one side of the net from the bund.

The prawns harvested are put into a cage in the pool for the first sorting and to remove the soft shelled ones if they are not saleable.

In the discontinuous system, prawns are harvested by draining the pond. This is carried out in the early morning to avoid overheating the water when there is only a little water left. At the final stage when the prawns are near the outlet, they must be provided with fresh oxygenated water near the outlet channel to attract them. Fresh water must never be let in at the top of the pool since this would cause the prawns to go back to the top against the current.

91

10 Marketing

10.1 *Processing and packing*

Processing prawns after harvesting is a vital stage in preserving the product's organoleptic and healthy qualities. As soon as a prawn dies, enzymes released at ambient temperature by the hepatopancreas and bacteria in the environment rapidly begin to break down the proteins in the muscles. This breakdown starts at the cephalothorax and spreads to the end of the tail. The result is that the flesh loses its firmness and when cooked it becomes woolly. Since enzyme activity is inhibited by low temperature, it is very important to adhere to the following procedure immediately after harvesting.

The prawns are killed by immersion in tanks of iced water at the edge of the pool. The tanks are then taken to the on-farm processing area, where the prawns are put into containers of clean water and melting ice for 30 minutes.

After cooling, which stops enzyme activity, the prawns are quickly sorted and packed for sale. This is either done on the farm or in a special building to which they are taken in insulated containers with ice (1 kg ice for 1 kg prawns), taking care never to have several layers of prawns and not to allow them to be immersed in water from the melting ice.

The following methods of packing are used.

- Prawns to be sold fresh are packed in 2.5 kg insulated boxes with ice in sealed plastic bags or gel packs. Fresh prawns must be eaten within five days.
- Prawns to be sold frozen; in this case there are two methods:
  * soaking in brine at −20°C. The brine contains maize syrup which prevents the prawns from adhering to each other after freezing.
  * using a freezing tunnel – the glazing technique – by vaporising water during freezing to avoid desiccation of the surface of the carapace.

The brine method appears to be the most suitable for prawns.

All handling after harvesting and packing must be done with great care since the quality of the final product depends directly on this. The quality must be perfect to guarantee the product's good reputation.

10.2 Marketing the prawns

For a long time the only market for freshwater prawns was in the region where they were caught in their natural habitat. Freshwater prawns are very popular on islands where there are no sea prawns. They form an important ingredient of the local dishes.

Apart from these local markets, exports to the principal sea prawn consumer countries, USA, Japan and Europe came from the large natural resources of countries in southeast Asia. They were sold as a downmarket substitute for sea prawns and were packed in the same way, as tails in 2 kilogram blocks with no precise identification. Their low quality was due more to inferior packing (originally because freshwater prawns came from widely scattered areas in the different countries with no means of keeping them refrigerated from the time they were caught) rather than to the quality of the prawns themselves.

Prawn farming was first developed in the regions where prawns were known and appreciated. Marketing was based on the sale price of local freshwater prawns, which was very high because of their scarcity as a result of over-harvesting natural stocks. This was often associated with tourist development in such regions.

Other development programmes were started with a view to exporting to the principal consumer countries. There was competition for these markets from exports from countries in southeast Asia, where since the middle of the 1980s treatment and packing have been improving to the point where the whole product, properly identified, is processed.

This competition was felt, particularly in regions where production costs were high, such as Puerto Rico and French Guiana. In view of the competition, marketing policies were implemented to give a specific image to the farmed product. Three examples of branded products are:
- the Sabana Grande farm in Puerto Rico
- the New York freshwater prawn marketing enterprise 'Sweet Water Prawn, Inc.'
- the French Guiana Freshwater Prawn Producer Group.

The policy is to sell a high-quality product which will justify a high price.

Fig 49 *Advertising literature for marketing top quality freshwater prawns (photo: Denis Lacroix, IFREMER)*

The quality of these three products is superb and they have recognition value ('Caribbean Scampi', 'Sweet Water Prawn' or 'Blue Caribbean Sea Prawn'). When sold to the public, packs are accompanied by information giving the product's origin, characteristics (taste, texture and low cholesterol content) and recipes for the housewife. After being flown from the production centres, prawns are sold fresh to impress customers with their high quality and superiority over competitors' products.

Its popularity with hypermarkets, supermarkets and restaurants is an indication of a good future for the freshwater prawn.

SECTION 3
Penaeid shrimp farming

11 Penaeid shrimp farming – introduction

Penaeid shrimps have been farmed for a very long time in some parts of the world, where the technique is practised very simply on an extensive scale.

The development of new rearing techniques provided new impetus for this activity in the 1970s. The farming of some species of penaeid shrimps has now become a very important activity in certain tropical countries. These countries, where the environment and economics are often very favourable, have been able to adapt to technological progress rapidly and effectively.

One of these countries is Ecuador, where this form of specialised aquatic farming has developed very rapidly, making use of the large numbers of young shrimps found in their natural surroundings, and marginal areas that are unsuitable for agriculture. After a stage during which development took place without any form of control, the structure of this pioneering industry has improved slightly; shrimp farming has now matured to a certain extent and is endeavouring to be less dependent on the natural environment and concentrate on improving yields. As a result, the number of hatcheries has increased – although not without problems – and compound feeds manufactured locally have been improved, so that farms can be gradually intensified. The market, which for a long time was principally the USA, is becoming increasingly diversified.

The situation is similar in the case of Taiwan, where the boom in marine shrimp farming, which is even more recent (and extraordinary), is the result of an intensive sector which initially modelled itself on shrimp farming in Japan.

New producer countries, such as mainland China, Thailand and Mexico, are already appearing.

The proportion of farm production in the world's total production has increased rapidly, reaching nearly 25 per cent in 1988.

However, it was in 1988 that the first serious problems of disease appeared in both Thailand and Ecuador. These countries now apparently expend an enormous amount of energy with a total lack of organisation and little regard for the natural environment. The use of different techniques has led to a de facto increase in the risk of disease and the proximity – or even overlapping – of production units has made contamination more likely.

It is difficult to write a document such as this, since techniques now have to be described against a background of particularly sensitive situations which might ultimately cast doubt on some production systems themselves. This crisis will, however, almost certainly make it possible for new progress to be made in technology and, in particular, with more regard for the environment.

12 Biology

12.1 *Classification, morphology, distribution*

Penaeid shrimps form a very old group of Decapod crustaceans found principally in the sea, although some species live in estuaries. Penaeids belong to the Arthropod sub-kingdom, Crustacea class, Malacostracan group, Eucharid sub-class, Decapod order, Natantia sub-order, Penaeid family, *Penaeus* genus.

The genus *Penaeus* may be distinguished from the genus *Macrobrachium* (*caridae* section) by its morphological and biological characteristics. In the case of penaeid shrimps the anterior edge of each abdominal segment is covered by the carapace of the previous segment. In the *Macrobrachium* eggs are carried on the abdominal legs during embryo development, while in penaeids they develop internally in the ovary. In addition, penaeids lay many more eggs than *Macrobrachium* shrimps.

Fig. 50   *Penaeus monodon*

There are more than 300 species of penaeid shrimps, which are found mainly in warm or temperate seas. Most species live in areas of shallow water. They are found in an area bounded more or less by the 20° **isotherm**, which is the temperature of the surface water in summer.

Table 9 gives the most important commercial species, their location and common names (according to the FAO).

Table 9 Commercial species, locations and common names

Species	Common name	Location
Penaeus semisulcatus	Green tiger prawn	Indian Ocean/Pacific Ocean
Penaeus merguiensis	Banana prawn	Indian Ocean/Pacific Ocean
Penaeus indicus	Indian white prawn	Indian Ocean/Pacific Ocean
Penaeus monodon	Giant tiger prawn	Indian Ocean/Pacific Ocean
Penaeus japonicus	King prawn Kuruma ebi	Indian Ocean/Pacific Ocean
Penaeus orientalis	Fleshy prawn	Indian Ocean/Pacific Ocean
Penaeus latisulcatus	Western king prawn	Indian Ocean/Pacific Ocean
Penaeus esculentus	Brown tiger prawn	Indian Ocean/Pacific Ocean
Penaeus notialis	Northern pink shrimp	East Atlantic
Penaeus setiferus	Northern white shrimp	West Atlantic
Penaeus duorarum	Northern pink shrimp	West Atlantic
Penaeus aztecus	Northern brown shrimp	West Atlantic
Penaeus subtilis	Southern brown shrimp	West Atlantic
Penaeus schmitti	Southern white shrimp	West Atlantic
Penaeus brasiliensis	Redspotted shrimp	West Atlantic
Penaeus californiensis	Yellowleg shrimp	East Pacific
Penaeus vannamei	Whiteleg shrimp	East Pacific
Penaeus stylirostris	Blue shrimp	East Pacific
Penaeus brevirostris	Crystal shrimp	East Pacific
Penaeus occidentalis	Western white shrimp	East Pacific
Penaeus kerathurus	Caramote prawn	Mediterranean and East Atlantic

12.2 Life cycle

There are four stages in the life cycle of penaeid shrimps, characterised by changes in morphology and considerable changes in behaviour and environment.

Phase 1   Reproduction

This generally takes place in the sea, in waters 20 to 30 metres deep. Mating very often takes place at dusk. Without going into details of

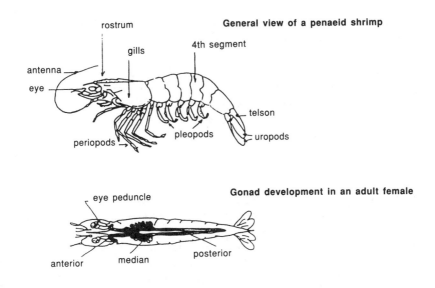

General view of a penaeid shrimp

Gonad development in an adult female

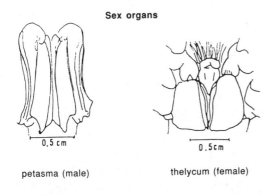

Sex organs

petasma (male)

thelycum (female)

Fig. 51 *The penaeid shrimp*

the reproductive systems, two groups of species may be distinguished by the shape of the female sex organ, the **thelycum**.

- Species with a closed thelycum in which mating takes place after moulting: egg laying may take place several days or even several weeks later. In this case the sacs, known as spermatophores, which contain the spermatozoa are deposited in the thelycum of the female.
- Species with an open thelycum which mate when the ovarium is ripe: this occurs only a few hours before laying, the spermatozoa being deposited on the outside of the thelycum.

99

In both cases eggs are fertilised the moment they are expelled, then dispersed into the water. Providing the temperature is favourable, they hatch in about 12 hours. Females lay several hundred thousand eggs, numbers depending on the size of the animal. The first stage of larval development, the nauplius, appears at hatching.

This stage, which consists of six sub-stages, lasts for two to three days during which the larva does not feed. The nauplius, which swims using its appendages, is attracted to the light, i.e. to the surface.

Phase 2   Larval development

The following two larval stages are known as zoea and mysis. They last for eight to ten days in all and are characterised by considerable anatomical and physiological changes.

The zoea has a digestive tract and feeds on very small phytoplanktonic algae. This stage lasts for about four days.

The mysis begins to resemble a small shrimp although it moves in jerks with its head down. It rapidly becomes carnivorous and eats its prey (zooplankton) alive. After it has metamorphosed for the last time, it enters the post-larval stage and has the morphology and behaviour of a shrimp. It swims horizontally but can also swim downwards. At this stage, which lasts from several weeks to several months, some species begin to migrate to coastal waters and lagoons of brackish water.

Phase 3   The juvenile stage

Young shrimps, or juveniles, spend some time in estuaries or coastal bays. Some species are more often found in these areas of shallow, brackish, often muddy waters, where it appears that they find plenty of food. After some weeks they go back to the coastal areas and deeper waters.

The habitat, behaviour and food of juveniles vary considerably according to the species. All young shrimps are, however, very active at night, searching for food, moulting or moving about. They are less active by day and move very slowly; some species even hide.

Phase 4   Adult stage

When their sexual characteristics appear; young shrimps have the morphology of adults and a few months later become sexually mature.

Information relating to the life and type of habitat of marine shrimps is very often incomplete, even non-existent in the case of many species. During growth sexual dimorphism is often observed; it is more apparent in some species than others. Adult females are generally larger than males.

Growth is linked to the moult cycle. Moulting always occurs, its frequency varying according to body weight and certain physical and chemical parameters in the environment. Moulting is controlled by a hormone which is secreted as a result of external stimulation (photoperiodism, increase in water temperature, etc.).

Growth varies very considerably according to environmental conditions and also according to the species. Some species have been selected for culture because of their fast growth rates under conditions of captivity, even where the stocking density is sometimes very high. Four species deserve mention – *Penaeus monodon*, *Penaeus vannamei*, *Penaeus stylirostris* and *Penaeus japonicus*.

Juveniles of 20 to 40 days of age can reach an average weight of over 20 g in four to six months.

Several factors influence growth during rearing. These are principally water temperature, salinity, food quality and density. Temperature appears to be the most important factor for some species such as *Penaeus monodon*. It has been found that the growth rate of this species at a temperature of 28°C was twice as fast as at 24.5°C; it was almost nil at below 22°C.

There is also an optimum salinity, which is generally below that of normal seawater salinity (35 parts per thousand, or 35‰). Some species are, however, more marine than others. For example, excellent rearing results are obtained with *Penaeus japonicus* at a salinity of between 3.0 and 3.6 per cent while *Penaeus monodon* gives better results at 1.5 to 2.5 per cent.

Food also plays an important part. The considerable amount of research work carried out in recent years has shown that nutritional requirements vary very considerably according to species. Consequently, there is no one feed for shrimps, but a feed suitable for each species, even specifically for the performance expected from these species on farms. Moreover, formulae for feeds for extensive or semi-extensive units are simpler than those for intensive units. In the first case natural production will in fact make up for any deficiencies in compound feeds (vitamins, trace elements, fatty acids, etc.), while for intensive systems the compound must provide all the nutrients required for growth.

Since nutritional requirements vary according to species, the type of feed, and therefore the cost of feeding, varies very considerably. Since feed is the most costly item on a farm, this is a very important aspect. The following examples illustrate the different feed requirements for one farm with the same stocking density but different species:

- *Penaeus japonicus* – a diet with 60 per cent protein
- *Penaeus monodon* – a diet with 40 per cent protein
- *Penaeus vannamei* and *Penaeus stylirostris* – a diet with 30 per cent protein.

Feed for *Penaeus japonicus* will probably cost four to six times as much as feed for *Penaeus vannamei*.

The density, or stocking rate, is also a factor whose influence on growth varies very considerably according to species.

Under optimum rearing conditions some species will very quickly reach a growth threshold at a weight which is often inadequate to satisfy market requirements. In others, the growth threshold will be reached when the shrimps are of marketable size, even when the stocking density is very high. For example, *Penaeus indicus* will very quickly reach its maximum growth rate at a weight of 10–12 g at a stocking density of 5–15 shrimps/m^2, while *Penaeus vannamei* will easily reach a weight of 20 g at over 100 shrimps/m^2. The growth potential of a species will therefore depend not only on the characteristics of the species, but also on its performance under specific rearing conditions, and therefore on the skill of the farmer.

13 Sites suitable for shrimp farming

13.1 General

The correct siting of a unit is of paramount importance. A site must therefore be studied carefully, taking into consideration the following factors and conditions.

Climate

- air temperature (average, minimum, maximum, daily range)
- rainfall (distribution, frequency, amount, thunderstorms, storms)
- wind(direction, seasonal variations, force)
- relative humidity

Water and the environment

- physical: currents, swell, tidal range, temperature and salinity variations (daily, seasonal), turbidity
- chemical: pH, dissolved gases and elements, presence of toxic compounds (heavy metals, pesticides, hydrocarbons, etc.)
- bacteriological

Other factors

- availability of fresh water:
  * river (flow and seasonal variation)
  * groundwater (depth of water table, presence of bore holes or wells)
- biological environment:
  * natural **productivity** (apparent primary and secondary production, photosynthesis)

* presence of penaeid shrimps in the natural environment (identification, stage, frequency of observation)
* risk of **eutrophication**, **dystrophy**

Land characteristics

- soil type (nature, texture, plasticity)
- permeability
- particle size
- acidity and potential acidity, i.e. toxicity
- general topography (average level above high tide, general slope)
- risk of flooding
- the shore (nature of ground, stability of coast line, depth of water)

Socio-economic conditions

- accessibility, distance from urban centres (ports and airports)
- land use
- availability of labour
- electricity, telex, telephone

Local costs

- land
- construction costs (terracing, civil engineering)
- equipment costs (pumps, tanks, filters, etc.)

Fig 52   *Constructing ponds in China*

The region

- population
- agriculture, industry
- pollution risks (industrial, domestic, agricultural, other shrimp farms, mining)

Restrictions

- legal
- competition for space and water utilisation
- possible expansion

A site must be studied not only to determine its suitability for shrimp farming but also to determine the modifications and preparation necessary to set up a realistic project. A site must therefore always be studied with a view to developing it so that the person conducting the study should have had experience of this type of work.

Three stages are necessary when conducting a study.

1 Examination of existing documents to obtain preliminary information on the environment as well as logistic and economic factors (information on climatic and economic aspects, maps, satellite photographs, etc.)

2 Visits to the site, investigating it to complement information obtained previously: During this stage it is often essential first to fly over the area to obtain a view of the whole site in relation to its surroundings.

Fig 53 *Nursery tanks at the Inbiosa hatchery (Ecuador)*

Fig 54 *A semi-intensive farm in Ecuador*

3 Taking observations and measurements in situ (water quality, soil, general topography, etc.) to provide the basic data required for preparing the project study.

The criteria used in selecting a farm for an intensive unit will not be exactly the same as those for a semi-intensive farm. Each type of farm is subject to certain constraints. When selecting a site for a hatchery, the factors to be taken into consideration are more specific.

13.2 *Selection of a site for a hatchery*

A hatchery is a number of units involved in the production of post-larvae. The building in which these units are generally housed is known as the hatchery. In addition to small tanks for broodstock and nurseries, other buildings, such as offices, workshops and houses often have to be included in a hatchery project. Space must therefore be allowed for all these. When choosing a site, the following factors must be taken into consideration.

Environmental conditions

Extreme temperatures, the direction of prevailing winds, frequency of rainfall and the amount of sun must all be considered when siting the building, choosing its orientation and deciding whether or not to insulate certain parts of it, how to ventilate it, whether to use air conditioning etc.

106

Fig 55   *An intensive rearing pond, Aquacop, Tahiti*

Water quality is of paramount importance for a hatchery site. The characteristics of pumped water must be as near as possible to those of sea water, i.e:

- constant salinity between 3.0 and 3.6 per cent
- a temperature of above 25°C and below 30°C (this is obviously only found in the tropics, in other regions a heating system must be installed)
- a pH of about 8.2.

When setting up the pumping station, and especially when choosing the type of pumping, account must be taken of currents, swell, height of tides, depth of water and stability of the coastline. Particular attention should be paid to water quality and the possibility of pollution (proximity of industries, intensive agriculture, domestic waste).

Insecticides, pesticides, hydrocarbons and heavy metals have an adverse effect on shrimp larvae, even at low concentrations, e.g. a few micrograms of Cu^{2+} per litre will cause necrosis.

The geography of the site and use of the hinterland should also be considered. Although a hatchery does not require a very large area (only a few hectares), the following should nevertheless not be forgotten:

- the actual available area (frequent competition with other activities along the coast) and cost of land
- access to pumping and conditions for disposing of waste
- topography (level, only slightly raised to reduce pumping costs)
- soil quality (stable and impervious if it is planned to construct earthwork ponds for broodstock).

107

Logistic and economic conditions

In order to obtain the water required it is often necessary to build hatcheries at some distance from the farms.

One of the important factors is accessibility. A hatchery must be easily accessible from an urban centre to reduce the cost of:
- bringing in electricity and/or fuel
- obtaining spare parts and carrying out general maintenance
- obtaining small items of consumable goods (fresh food, *Artemia*, medicines and chemicals).

Living conditions for the staff must also be considered.

The hatchery must be able to deliver post-larvae to the rearing unit easily, in a reasonably short time. Some means of communication, such as telephone or telex, is therefore desirable. Labour should also be available near the site.

When assessing investment costs, account must be taken not only of purchasing the land but also the cost of preliminary studies, and especially of acquiring the necessary technology.

13.3   *Selection of a farm site*

Two systems must be considered.

- **Intensive**: The area required may only be 20 or 30 hectares or less. Ninety per cent of all intensive shrimp farms now keep *Penaeus monodon*. On intensive farms this species requires the following:
  * for rearing, preferably brackish water with a salinity of 1.53.
  * high quality feed
  * an aeration system.

  Since some requirements of intensive farms, e.g. food quality and maintenance, cannot always be satisfied, the choice of a site depends on conditions in general, with logistics and the availability of brackish water (a mixture of fresh and sea water) as the principal factors.
- **Extensive or semi-intensive**: The main factor is the area available. Farms of this type generally cover large areas (several hundred hectares). Water quality requirements are less demanding, although brackish water is always preferable. This system allows greater flexibility; accessibility, delays in supplying feed or minor pumping problems do not put the farm at risk.

The conditions generally required for setting up a sea farm for saltwater shrimps should be examined as a whole.

Climatic conditions

The best climate for marine shrimp farming is similar to that in the tropics, i.e:
- an air temperature between 25 and 30°C, with a minimum of annual variations and very small daily range
- average rainfall distributed throughout the year
- steady winds from the same direction and at below force 4 on the Beaufort scale
- no storms, torrential rain or cyclones.

Obviously, these requirements are rarely all met. A typical climate often has two alternating seasons – cold and dry then hot and humid – or periods of drought followed by heavy rainfall at certain times. In this case particular attention should be paid to studying problems arising from variations in salinity, flooding and erosion of bunds.

Water characteristics

The pumping possibilities must first be studied, taking into consideration the height of tides, depth of water, currents and coastal stability.

Protected channels, where the water is replaced by the tides, are often good places to obtain water. However, in tropical areas with a long dry season and where the **tidal range** is insufficient, a large volume of water may be trapped in the channels and become quickly hypersalinate as the result of evaporation. Large estuaries with many

---

The principal water quality characteristics desired are as follows:
- temperature: 24–32°C (optimum 28°C)
- salinity: 1.0–3.5‰ varying according to the species of shrimp*
- pH: 7.5–8.8
- dissolved oxygen: never less than 3 ppm
- iron: under 2 ppm
- ammonia: less than 0.3 mg NH_3–N/litre (non-ionised)
- nitrites: less than 6 mg NO_2–N/litre
- nitrates: less than 100 mg NO_3–N/litre.

* Growth is optimum in full-strength sea water (36‰) for most species of penaeid shrimp. However, some species, such as *Penaeus japonicus*, *Penaeus schmitti* and *Penaeus stylirostris*, are unaffected by salinity between 3.5 and 3.8‰.

channels nevertheless may provide suitable sites. The water in them is very often brackish for a large part of the year. Furthermore, fresh water flowing in generally contains minerals and nutrients which are natural fertilisers.

Problems arising from bacterial action are less obvious since an organism which is pathogenic to man is not necessarily so to shrimps. Nevertheless, areas contaminated by domestic effluent should be avoided.

Fresh water requirements vary more or less according to the level of intensity of culture. If pumped water on intensive farms using *Penaeus monodon* has a relatively high salinity, groundwater resources should be evaluated in order to mix the two if possible. Apart from this, fresh water is used mainly for washing equipment and sometimes before packing the shrimps.

The quality of the biological environment should also be assessed. It is useful to have good natural productivity since natural products play an important part in feeding shrimps, especially on extensive systems.

The presence of filtering molluscs, fish and shrimps in the natural environment is an asset. Large quantities of shrimp post-larvae of the species desired may be found in the natural environment, often seasonally. If this is so, it may not be necessary to start a hatchery at once since a regular supply of wild post-larvae may be available, at a reasonable cost of course.

It is also sometimes possible to catch adult shrimps in the area in which the project is planned. However, in most cases the supply is irregular as a result of fluctuations in the population owing to migration. Care must be taken not to exploit wild stocks. Moreover, in some parts of the world it may be illegal to catch either mature adults or post-larvae from the wild, at least at certain times of the year.

The terrain and soil

The general topography of the site must be carefully examined since it is important to have a large flat area slightly above sea level. Three types of terrain may be distinguished.

1 The intertidal area
In tropical countries there is often a mangrove swamp in the **intertidal** area. In Asia this area is often used for traditional aquatic farming[1], making use of the tide to fill and drain the ponds. Apart from the

1 Indonesian 'Tambak'

110

fact that yields obtained from this type of farming are only mediocre, there are two major disadvantages to using these areas:
- The destruction of a mangrove swamp may in time result in an imbalance of the ecosystem and repercussions on the natural fish and crustacean stocks.
- The soil in mangrove swamps generally has a high sulphuric acid potential. Complex chemical reactions occur resulting in marked acidification of the soil, which is aggravated by deforestation and terracing.

Acidification has a direct effect on farmed shrimps and very high mortality is common after heavy rainfall when water runs down the pond bunds carrying the very acid surface soil with it.

Acidification also harms the fauna and flora, the natural food of shrimps. Great care should therefore be taken when choosing this system, even if running costs appear very reasonable.

Table 10   Characteristics of mangrove swamp soils

	Acid soils	Normal soils
pH	3.5	7.2
Aluminium (ppm)	230	trace
Iron	110	25
Sulphates	1500	550
Phosphates	14	10

2   Flat, saline areas

The flat, saline areas are generally alluvial with no vegetation, at the extreme top of the tidal area, known as 'tannes' or 'salitrales' in Latin America.

These predominantly clay areas generally have a much lower acid potential than those of the mangrove swamps. When large ponds are constructed, covering several hectares and fed by pumping, there is little or no change in the existing soil which forms the bottom of the pond. The use of these areas has hardly any adverse effect on the environment since either the terrain is not altered or the project is adapted to the topography and, in particular, to the natural drainage.

However, since water has to be pumped to a site of this nature, a semi-intensive system must be used (higher density, use of compound feeds, etc.), which is much more costly than a traditional extensive system and therefore can hardly be considered as anything but a commercial undertaking.

3 Clay/silt coastal plains

The clay/silt coastal plains above the level of the highest tides are areas that can also be used as sites for farms, provided that they are not marshy.

These coastal plains are generally covered with woodland and/or used for agriculture. In this case the cost of the land has to be taken into consideration, while the 'tannes' normally have a very low market value since they have no particular use.

In short, the first type of land is more suitable for traditional extensive aquatic farming. The second type is that of the large semi-intensive farms, e.g. in Ecuador. The third is more suitable for intensive farms because of their limited area and better accessibility, e.g. Taiwan.

In all cases the soil should be examined to see if it is suitable for constructing compacted earth ponds.

Since predominantly clay soils are the most desirable, samples are taken and analysed to determine:
- their nature and uniformity
- plasticity
- particle size
- permeability
- pH.

During the preliminary stage while a detailed survey is being carried out, measurements will be taken to assess the possibilities of compacting (Proctor index).

13.4 *Economic conditions*

In addition to the purely biotechnical aspects, the economic feasibility of a project should be evaluated, especially:
- the cost of land (and possible legal limitations)
- construction costs including those of any waste treatment ponds or facilities that may be deemed necessary
- accessibility (construction of roads if necessary)
- availability and cost of local labour
- the supply of consumables (energy/fuel)
- the processing and removal of the finished product.

A feasibility study can be prepared from this information.

Costs vary very considerably according to the country and complexity of the project. As an indication, the next table shows the proportions of the investment required for setting up a large semi-intensive farm in Latin America.

Table 11 Proportion of the cost of principal items in relation to total investment

Semi-intensive farm (200 to 500 hectares)	
Principal items	**% of total**
Terracing	46%
Civil and hydraulic engineering	9%
Pumping station	18%
Buildings and housing	7%
Electrical equipment	5%
Other equipment (workshop, harvesting, scientific, vehicles)	15%
	100%

The cost per hectare of a complete farm is between US$8000 and US$15 000 depending on the site and country. For an intensive farm the cost may be as high as US$50 000 per hectare.

The investment necessary for building a commercial hatchery to produce between 50 and 250 million post-larvae per year is generally between US$8000 and US$12 000 per million post-larvae produced.

Processing is carried out in a special unit. The cost of processing is generally about US$0.5–0.7 per kg of shrimps.

The total production cost of a kilogram of shrimps on a semi-intensive unit is between US$3 and US$4.

Table 12 The proportions of running costs to total costs (apart from financial charges)

Charges	%
Post-larvae (purchased)	15–25
Food	30–50
Fertiliser	3–5
Labour	10–15
Fuel	5–15
Maintenance	3–5
Depreciation	10–15

Table 13 Comparison of some important aspects of three farming systems used for the same species (*Penaeus vannamei*)

	Extensive	Semi-intensive	Intensive
Source of juveniles	natural environment	natural environment or hatchery using wild broodstock	hatchery and rearing broodstock in captivity
Cost of post-larvae per 1000 post-larvae	US$3–10	US$5–15	US$5–15
Stocking density Shrimps/m²	0.5–2	5–15	100
Average pond area (ha)	0.5–20	1–20	0.15–0.5
Water replacement	tide (day/month) pumping (less than 2% per day)	pumping 2–100% per day	pumping 10–50% per day
Aeration	none	none	20 HP/ha
Food	produced naturally	compound food 25–35% protein	compound food 30–40% protein
Food cost	nil	US$0.50–0.70 per kg	US$0.70–1.00 per kg
Food conversion ratio	nil	1.3–2.5	2.5–3.5
Survival rate from P20	50%	40–80%	70–80%
Annual yield	0.2–0.6 t/ha	1–4/ha	18–25 t/ha
Weight reach on unit (6 months)	20–30 g	18–22 g	20 g
Ex-farm production cost	Below US$1.50 per kg	US$3–6 per kg	US$10–15 per kg

Fig 56 *A hatchery in Malaysia*

Fig 57   *A penaeid shrimp hatchery, Saint Vincent, New Caledonia*

14 Choice of species and system

When starting a shrimp farm the most important factors to be considered are first the species then the system.

14.1 *The species*

Many aspects must be considered when choosing a species:
- those of a purely biological nature (reproduction method, weight reached, number of eggs laid)
- those relating primarily to the species under farming conditions (growth rate, survival, etc.)
- finally, adequate knowledge of the species. Information is now available on several species which can be farmed.

Table 14 Distribution of species used for aquatic farming

Species	Temperate zone	Tropical zone				
	Warm	Asia	Africa	Pacific	The Caribbean	Latin America
Penaeus japonicus	+					
Penaeus monodon		+	+	+		
Penaeus indicus		+	+	+		
Penaeus stylirostris		+	+	+	+	+
Penaeus vannamei		+	+	+	+	+
Penaeus merguiensis		+	+	+		
Penaeus orientalis	+	+	+	+	+	+
Penaeus schmitti					+	+

The geographical region concerned and the presence of a suitable species in the region are obviously also determining factors. However, it is now possible to contemplate shrimp farming in favourable regions in some parts of the world where the species desired does not

Table 15 Characteristics of some species of *Penaeus* in farms

Species	Optimum temperature	Ease of handling	Protein content	Farm system	Average weight reached in 150 days from 1 g	Disadvantages
P. monodon	25–32°	Good	35–45%	extensive semi-intensive intensive	30–100 g 25–30 g 20–40 g	Requires high quality food
P. stylirostris	20–30°	Not so good	30–35%	extensive semi-intensive	30–40 g 20–30 g	Sensitive to environmental conditions
P. vannamei	24–32°	Average	30–35%	extensive semi-intensive intensive	30–35 g 15–22 g 15–22 g	Relatively small
P. merguiensis	22–32°	Poor	40–50%	extensive semi-intensive intensive	15–30 g 3.5 g 1.5 g	Relatively small
P. japonicus	18–28°	Very good	>60%	extensive semi-intensive	20–40 g 15–25 g	Expensive food
P. indicus	22–32°	Good	40–45%	extensive semi-intensive	20–30 g 8–12 g	Fair size only
P. orientalis	14–30°	Quite good	35–45%	extensive semi-intensive intensive	25–35 g 18–25 g 12–14 g	Little research so far into breeding in captivity

occur. Provided regulations allow, and the disease-free status of the stock can be guaranteed, then the species may be introduced and the broodstock reared in captivity. This is now possible for most of the above species since a rearing technique has been developed at the IFREMER France Aquaculture farms in Tahiti and New Caledonia. There is of course a risk that if the broodstock dies the project will be lost. This does not detract, however, from the relevance of the option to large projects which have suitable technology.

Table 15 summarises some principal characteristics and performance outlines of these species.

The three species most commonly used in the world at present are:

- *Penaeus monodon* – principally in Asia
- *Penaeus vannamei* – principally in Latin America and the Pacific
- *Penaeus stylirostris* – principally in Latin America and the Pacific.

These species are used mainly because of the following characteristics they exhibit when farmed:

- fast growth rate and market weight achieved in under 6 months
- good tolerance to a wide range of salinity (from 2.0 to 4.0 per cent)
- suitability for temperature variations between 25 and 32°C
- suitability for rearing in ponds with clay bottoms
- good resistance to environmental conditions and highly suitable for farming (easy to handle and harvest)
- good market value.

Fig 58   *Algae culture room, Saint Vincent, New Caledonia*

Fig 59 *Building a hatchery, FEGA, Indonesia*

Fig 60 *Freshwater and marine shrimp farm, Aquacop, Tahiti*

The final weights of these species vary. *Penaeus monodon*, and to a lesser extent *Penaeus stylirostris*, reach weights 10–30 per cent higher than *Penaeus vannamei* under identical rearing conditions. On the other hand, the market value of *Penaeus vannamei* is slightly higher and the cost of food required is appreciably less than for *Penaeus monodon*.

Fig 61   *Pacific Oceanology Centre, Aquacop, IFREMER, Tahiti*

14.2 *Farming methods*

Basic systems

It is generally accepted that there are three possible farming systems, the basic characteristics of which are summarised below.

Extensive

This system is traditionally used in Asia (known as 'Tambak' in Indonesia) in earth ponds or lagoons which have been adapted as required. Little water replacement is necessary since this generally occurs naturally by the action of the tides.

Low stocking density (fewer than two shrimps/m^2) either in a monoculture or with other stock, e.g. fish (*Chanos chanos*), generally with no supplementary feeding. The natural cycle of production and breakdown of living material is allowed to continue at its optimum yield, which is sometimes increased by the use of fertilisers. Annual yields are less than 800 kilograms per hectare.

Semi-intensive

This system, which is widely used throughout Latin America, has now been perfected and is considered reliable. Large earthwork ponds are used with water inlets and outlets which, with the use of pumps, have proved to be a satisfactory means of replacing the water.

The average stocking densities are between 5 and 15 shrimps per square metre; a compound feed is given.

Annual yields, which depend on climatic conditions, stockmanship and the organisation of production cycles, are between two and four tonnes per hectare.

Intensive

The latest methods are used for this system. Rearing is in small areas (several thousand cubic metres) equipped with aeration systems. Three methods are used:

- the American 'raceway', based on a strong current of replacement water; annual yields of 20–30 tonnes per hectare are obtained from *Penaeus vannamei* and *Penaeus stylirostris*
- the Asian method, which is halfway between the semi-intensive and the hyper-intensive 'raceway' technique, is based on fast aeration, water replacement in sequence and the use of high performance foods; annual yields are between 6 and 20 tonnes per hectare for *Penaeus monodon*
- the French method (Aquacop), which is based on the recycling of farming waste by nitrifying bacteria, requires the use of compound feeds, a lot of aeration but little water replacement; annual yields of 20 to 30 tonnes per hectare are obtained from several species. This method is used on a commercial scale in French Polynesia.

The Asian method is currently used on a large scale, although both the Taiwanese and Thai industries – pioneers in intensive shrimp culture techniques – have recently moved back towards more extensive methods as a result of chronic disease and environmental problems. Production costs are generally higher than for the traditional semi-intensive system (the species used is *Penaeus monodon*) because:

- food is generally two to three times more expensive
- energy costs (for aeration) are higher, as are maintenance costs
- staff must be reliable and skilled.

The intensive system cannot be used everywhere and is increasingly less favoured because of disease and environmental problems. Extensive or semi-extensive systems may be profitable where sufficient areas of suitable land are available. Their use does not necessarily require considerable investment, particularly when a cheap simple compound feed is available locally.

Farming stages

There are three stages in shrimp farming: the larval stage, pre-rearing and rearing. Shrimp farming involves three stages:

- the larval stage in a hatchery
- pre-rearing in a nursery
- rearing in ponds to marketable size.

Rearing larvae

Larvae are reared in a hatchery, which consists of a number of units each with its own specific function, operating in conjunction with each other to ensure that post-larvae are produced regularly.

A hatchery consists of:
- ponds for holding broodstock
- a maturing area
- a spawning/hatching area
- a larva rearing room
- an algae production room
- an *Artemia* production unit.

In hatcheries, production periods are generally followed by rest periods for cleaning out.

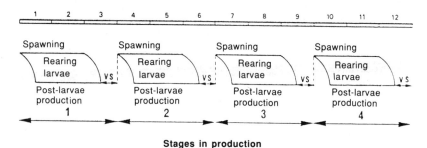

Stages in production

Fig 62   *Stages in production*

The units – broodstock rearing ponds

Problems with the rearing of broodstock have recently been overcome, principally by IFREMER at Tahiti and in New Caledonia. This technique is, however, not yet widely used, so most hatcheries obtain broodstock from the natural habitat. All stages of rearing generally take place in simple ponds generally made of earth. Shrimps are selected at the juvenile stage and are managed to ensure the production of healthy broodstock in as short a time as possible. Broodstock are either kept intensively, as in the case of *Penaeus vannamei*, or very extensively in the case of *Penaeus monodon*.

Maturing

Shrimps are put in round tanks at a maximum stocking density of 300 g/m^2 and are fed on fresh feed and special compound feeds.

Table 16 Broodstock production

	Initial stocking rate (per m²)	Time (months)	Collection/selection
Stage 1	4.5	4	1/3
Stage 2	1.5	4	1/3
Stage 3	0.5	4	1/3
Total		12	

The temperature is kept between 27°C and 30°C.
Maturity and spawning occur quite soon after unilateral eye stalk removal. This process removes the gland which produces hormones that inhibit spawning. Each female can lay up to three times a month.

Spawning and hatching
Females ready to spawn are isolated in small circular conical-bottomed tanks. Spawning generally takes place at night and the eggs collected on filters are put into incubators. Hatching occurs several hours later and the nauplii are collected and taken directly to the larval rearing tanks.

Larval rearing

Larvae are reared in circular conical-bottomed or U-shaped tanks, the size of which varies according to production capacity (between 1 m³ and 15 m³). This intensive technique is illustrated later in a simplified form.

Algae production
Single-celled algae are used as food for shrimp larvae at the zoea stage. They must be of suitable size, multiply rapidly and be readily accepted by the larvae.
Only strains of algae selected and tested previously are cultivated. A specific procedure must be carefully followed in algae production, which involves producing successive blooms of increasing size.

Artemia production
Artemia are small crustaceans which the shrimps catch alive. Artemia cysts can be stored and used as required. Hatching occurs in 24 or 36 hours and the nauplii produced are fed directly to the shrimp larvae. However, cyst quality varies very considerably, the number of eggs per gram generally being between 100 000 and 300 000 and the hatching rate between 30 and 80 per cent.

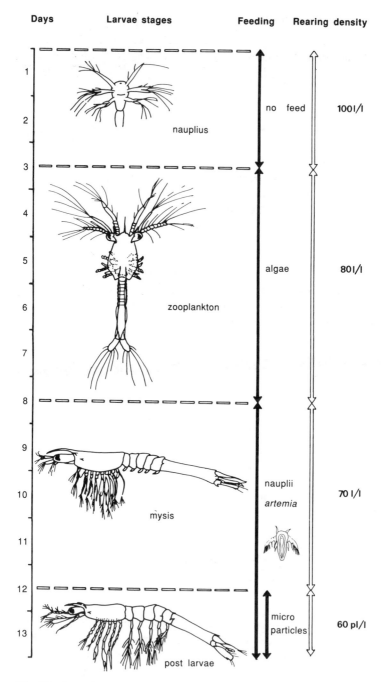

Days	Larvae stages	Feeding	Rearing density

nauplius

no feed — 100 l/l

zooplankton

algae — 80 l/l

mysis

nauplii *artemia* — 70 l/l

post larvae

micro particles — 60 pl/l

Fig 63 *Larval stages*

124

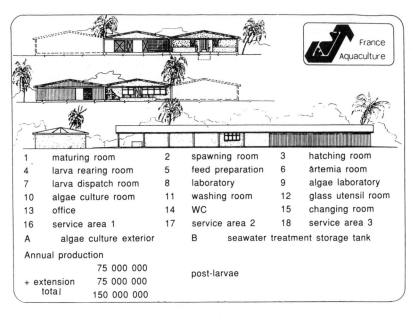

1	maturing room	2	spawning room	3	hatching room
4	larva rearing room	5	feed preparation	6	artemia room
7	larva dispatch room	8	laboratory	9	algae laboratory
10	algae culture room	11	washing room	12	glass utensil room
13	office	14	WC	15	changing room
16	service area 1	17	service area 2	18	service area 3
A	algae culture exterior	B	seawater treatment storage tank		

Annual production

	75 000 000	post-larvae
+ extension	75 000 000	
total	150 000 000	

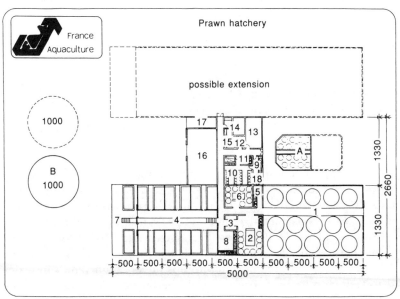

Fig 64 *France Agriculture – a shrimp hatchery*

Pre-rearing

This is a stage between the hatchery and the true rearing stage. It has two advantages:

- Rearing ponds can be stocked with a known number of juveniles. The risk of mortality at this stage is low. The stock in the pond can be more effectively monitored, especially for estimating feed requirements.
- It enables the farm to be managed more rationally. The pre-rearing stage shortens the rearing stage, thus enabling the stock in the ponds to be rotated more quickly.

Different systems can be used, with the stage lasting between ten days and two months and the average weight reaching 0.05–1 g. Two types of pre-rearing may be distinguished:

a traditional intensive pre-rearing in earthwork ponds of 1000–5000 m^2 with no aeration (stocking density 80 to 150 post-larvae/m^2). In this type the more zooplankton in the pond, the faster the growth rate. Conversion ratios on well managed units are below 2.

b hyper-intensive pre-rearing in small volumes of water with considerable aeration. The present trend is for short cycle pre-rearing periods (10–20 days), known as nursery stages.

The best pre-rearing results are obtained under the following conditions:

- post-larvae in good condition on stocking
- temperature between 26°C and 30°C
- salinity between 2.5 and 3.5 per cent
- batch stocking with one species
- use of good quality feed (frozen artemia, micro-particles).

Rearing

As has already been seen, there are several rearing methods; the method used depends on the stocking rate. Rearing ponds are generally of earth constructed on a level surface. Bunds are of compacted earth, constructed either by excavating and building up or by bringing in earth. Ponds are rarely excavated for three reasons:

- Since the land is generally low-lying (higher land is normally used for agriculture, and therefore is of very high value) in order to reduce pumping costs, it would be impossible to drain ponds by gravity.
- In view of the amount of excavation required, construction costs would be very high.
- Pond excavation in acid sulphate soils exposes the soil to the air, thereby oxidising sulphate compounds to form sulphuric acid and aggravating low pH conditions (see below).

Each pond is supplied with water through pipes from a pumping station, or more often through a channel. Water comes in and goes out through devices known as monks, which consist of filter screens and a flow regulation system.

The water is generally 0.8–1.5 m deep. The bottom of a pond is constructed so that draining takes place rapidly and the sediment

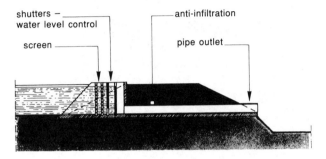

Section of a monk

View from above

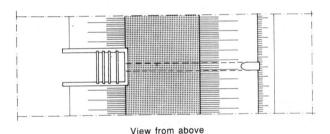

Section of a bund

Fig 65   *A monk*

Fig 66   *A drainage monk*

dries out. After drying, the pond bed may be harrowed to facilitate mineralisation of the organic matter. In the intensive system ponds are also provided with water aeration devices.

Culture conditions

Pond preparation
Preparation of the bed
Earth beds with a fairly high clay content or of heavy mud which become saturated with water are difficult to clean. The minimum drying time between two crops is about ten days. After the bed has dried out the soil must be aerated by using an implement such as a harrow or disc plough to enable the reduced organic material to be oxidised and pathogenic organisms to be destroyed. Aeration of the soil by harrowing is not recommended for very acid soils.

The pH of an acid soil may be improved by liming. The advantage of lime is that it disinfects and improves the soil structure by encouraging biological activity. A pond constructed of acid soil must be well washed before refilling.

Eliminating predators and competitors
If the bed and bunds of a pond are not properly dried, crabs, molluscs and fish found in wet areas should be killed. This is generally done using chlorine or rotenone. The number of predators (fish and crabs) and competitors (fish, molluscs and crustaceans) entering the pond

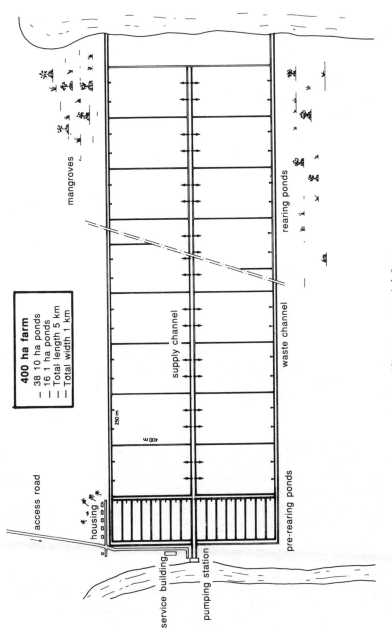

400 ha farm
- 38 10 ha ponds
- 16 1 ha ponds
- Total length 5 km
- Total width 1 km

access road

housing

mangroves

service building

pumping station

pre-rearing ponds

supply channel

250 m

400 m

waste channel

rearing ponds

Fig 67 *A commercial farm*

during rearing can be restricted by the use of screens at the water inlet monks. These fine mesh screens must be cleaned and checked several times a day.

Monitoring the environment and stock
The physical and chemical parameters and shrimps' natural food (plankton and **benthic** fauna) are closely related to the environment and its evolution. Natural productivity depends largely on the shrimps' feed and excreta, decomposition of the feed and other organic waste and the gradual mineralisation of the substrate. In order to avoid undesirable changes in the environment, it is important to be able to replenish large volumes of water and to control feeding and fertilising carefully.

Fertilising
The object of fertilising is to encourage the production of natural organisms which can be eaten by the shrimps and to increase the production of plankton, especially at the start of rearing when the biomass is small.

Organic fertilisers are used directly by **heterotrophic** bacteria and are subjected to the normal bacterial mineralisation cycle. Inorganic fertilisers are effective but may give rise to rapid phytoplankton blooms which are often unstable.

Several applications of fertiliser are recommended, especially during the first 15 days after filling. The total amount applied and frequency of application during rearing depends on the richness of the water, the soil and development of the environment. Inorganic fertilisers (which are only used in the water) dilute well if they are put in a bag at the water intake or in containers floating in the pond.

Control of the rearing environment
The rearing environment is controlled for two reasons:
- to maintain the natural productivity (phytoplankton, zooplankton, benthic production) of the environment
- to maintain the physical and chemical quality to ensure low mortality and good growth rates.

The principal means employed to control the environment are replenishment of the water and aeration.

When rearing commences, the water should be changed slowly and continually (0–10 per cent of the volume per day) increasing to 20–30 per cent per day at the end of rearing. It may, however, be necessary to change large amounts of water during the rearing period.

Aeration is used on intensive units. The object is to ensure that the level of dissolved oxygen is maintained; this should not fall below 3 mg/litre. For high density rearing (hyper-intensive) an algae and bacterial floc must be established in the environment. This floc plays an active part in the automatic removal of nitrogenous matter from waste produced, i.e. faeces and feed waste. To ensure success in an intensive system it is essential to maintain a balanced environment. The aeration system should be operating permanently since if it stops for a few hours at a critical time, the consequences could be serious.

DAILY CHECK
- dissolved oxygen (several times a day)
- pH
- temperature
- transparency, using a Secchi disc
- observation of colour (brownish-green) and appearance of the water (The colour is generally due to a mixture of different species of algae; this is always better than having one or two dominating species, when the bloom will be more unstable.)
- observation of behaviour (If the shrimps are not moving or come to the surface, there may be a temperature or oxygen problem. If they are continually swimming round the pond, there may be insufficient food.)
- cleaning the filter screens at the water inlet and outlet

Routine checks
By checking and observing the environment, changes can be detected and management adjusted accordingly.

Twice weekly checks
- ammonia, nitrates and nitrites
- observation of the stock for mortality, activity, moulting, disease, etc.

Monitoring the stock
The condition and growth of shrimps is monitored regularly by taking samples. Cages or cast nets of various types are used, while powered dragnets are used for *Penaeus japonicus*. Samples should be taken from several parts of the pond. The shrimps will be more uniformly distributed if they are not fed beforehand. In order to decide on

the amount of feed to be given, the number of shrimps must be estimated; this is done by estimating the average weight.

Numbers can be assessed by observing feed consumption over several days. Actual consumption – and from that the numbers – can be estimated from the proportion of food left from a given amount distributed. Numbers may also be assessed by marking and catching again later.

The number of shrimps must always be correctly assessed at the beginning of each rearing stage.

Shrimps are inspected at each sampling. The important aspects to be observed are:
- the colour and general appearance of the carapace
- firmness of the flesh
- absence of epiphytic algae, parasites, mould and necroses
- the condition of gills, appendages and antennae
- activity of the shrimps and regular moulting
- absence of dead shrimps at the bottom of the pond.

Feeding

When the stocking density is over 20 g/m^2, natural feed must be complemented by feed in pellet form. Two to three kilograms of pellets are required to produce a kilogram of shrimps of marketable size at a temperature of 20–25°C, the amount depending on the stocking density and food quality.

Most nutritional requirements during the first month are covered by natural production, but this production must be maintained by giving the compound feed from the beginning of rearing to prevent the natural food from being rapidly used up. Natural food plays an essential part in an extensive system.

Shrimps are active mainly at night. Pellets are manufactured so that they will remain in the water for several hours before breaking up. Feed given during the day is often not eaten for several hours, consequently it loses many of its nutrients. It is therefore better to give feed in the evening or at night. Feeding in the evening is adequate for low stocking densities (under 100 g/m^2); several feeds should be given daily where the density is higher.

Food must be scattered over as large an area of the pond as possible so that all the shrimps can feed.

The daily feed ration varies according to the shrimps' average weight and the temperature. There are still no precise rules relating to the effect of temperature on food consumption. There are, however, some guidelines, e.g. in the case of *Penaeus japonicus* at temperatures of 19–20°C the ration required is about half of that at 24–25°C; under 18°C only a minimal amount is required (0.5–1 per cent of the biomass every two to three days) since there is very little growth.

Feed requirements are calculated every week after sampling; sampling enables the biomass to be evaluated. The daily requirement is calculated by multiplying the biomass by a figure taken from a feed table, usually obtainable from a commercial feed manufacturer. This figure may have to be adjusted downwards to take temperature into account.

In all cases particular attention must be paid to food consumption; the calculation gives an average theoretical value which must be adjusted according to actual food consumption. Adjustment will generally be made downwards since shrimps are nearly always overfed.

Several handfuls may be thrown onto mosquito netting on the bottom at feeding time. If there are some pellets left when the netting is lifted in the morning, the ration must be reduced.

If food is always being left in the mosquito netting, it will be necessary to:
- examine the sediment carefully
- check the physical and chemical parameters
- check that there has been no exceptional mortality, which can be done by diving in the pond.

The principal environments encountered (according to Aquacop)

At the start of rearing there is sometimes a phytoplankton bloom, even when the stocking density is low and no fertiliser has been applied (the bloom uses minerals produced in the pond by mineralisation of the organic matter from the previous crop).

However, when a pond has just been stocked, i.e. when the stocking density is below 10–30 g/m², the first environment normally found is clear water, the characteristics of which are:
- disappearance of the Secchi disc at a depth of over 1 m
- a small amount of chlorophyll
- a pH of about 8.5.

There may be regular short periods of clear water during a rearing period after the sudden death of all phytoplankton. The water is then often a greyish or milky colour with a high bacterial load. A large volume of water is then replenished to encourage the regrowth of phytoplankton, reoxygenation and removal of possible toxic compounds such as ammonia.

This period of clear water may be accompanied by the growth of filamentous benthic algae, which are very difficult to remove.

The use of too much fertiliser during this period in order to encourage phytoplankton growth may lead to considerable growth of filamentous algae. This growth may also be associated with degradation of the bottom of the pond since the previous crop. These algae make it particularly difficult to harvest the shrimps and may also create problems during rearing (deterioration of the environment, **anoxic crises** and high mortality).

A small amount of water must be replenished to accelerate the appearance of phytoplankton, while at the same time a careful check must be kept to prevent stratification of the water (corrected by light aeration).

When the biomass increases, an environment of predominantly phytoplankton follows clear water. Typical features of this environment are:

- limited transparency
- high chlorophyll content
- a pH over 8.5
- oxygen content rising to a high level during the day (10–15 ppm) when there is no aeration or with slight aeration (introducing air results in degassing the super-saturated oxygen).

Phytoplankton density does not increase regularly in spite of the fact that there is some self-regulation of growth. In view of the limited light and mineral salt content, the phytoplankton population is subject to fluctuation.

It is principally the oxygen content which is affected physically and chemically by this change. This appears to be the only limiting factor which is apparent in these biomass conditions; only the phytoplankton can purify the pond properly, especially by eliminating ammonia.

In this type of environment the two principal questions which arise concerning its management are:

- whether the flow of water should be controlled to maintain the oxygen content at the desired level (over 3 mg/l) or whether aeration should be employed (The type of environment produced will depend on which method is used.)
- whether water should be supplied continuously or not (Changing water in sequence regenerates the phytoplankton blooms and leads to some moulting taking place at different times.)

The courses to be taken would depend on the experience of the farmer, i.e. his ability to evaluate all parameters relating to rearing and behaviour of the stock.

When the stocking density becomes high and under 20 per cent of the water is replaced per day, growth may no longer occur and the phytoplankton may not be sufficiently stable. The ammonia content may rise to around 5 mg/l NH_4-N. A floc of nitrifying bacteria may then appear, adding its purifying effect to that of the phytoplankton.

A nitrifying bacteria floc environment has the following characteristics:
- very limited transparency
- variable chlorophyll content
- a pH under 8.0
- low dissolved oxygen content during the day
- increasing nitrite content, then decreasing with the increase of nitrates.

A bacterial floc continually uses oxygen, unlike phytoplankton which produce oxygen during the day only.

In addition to monitoring oxygen content, particular attention should be paid to nitrogen salts, especially ammonia when it is increasing, which is just prior to establishment of the floc (the toxic form is not the NH^{4+} ion but un-ionised ammonia NH_3, the percentage of which depends on different factors, especially salinity and pH).

The NH_3-N content must not exceed 0.1 ppm. In order to conserve this type of environment, water replacement should not exceed a certain rate. This may mean that the farmer will have a difficult choice to make while ammonia is increasing. Bringing in fresh water to reduce the ammonia content also dilutes the growing floc (the appearance of nitrifying organisms may be encouraged by inoculation from a neighbouring active pond).

The last typical environment is a result of evolution of the phytoplankton environment, when there is a high density of shrimps and a replacement rate of over 30 per cent per day (or sequential). In this case there is no nitrifying bacteria floc but the density of heterotrophic bacteria becomes sufficiently high to cause a reduction in pH (due to the acidifying action of the CO_2) and prevent the daily increase in oxygen content when there is little aeration. The following will be apparent:
- the Secchi disc soon disappears
- a pH under 8.5
- stable dissolved oxygen content during the day
- absence of nitrogen salts (presence of phytoplankton).

Management of this environment depends primarily on oxygen content and involves altering the amount of water or air supplied.
- If insufficient water is replaced, a nitrifying floc may appear.
- If a lot of water is replaced, the density of heterotrophic bacteria will be reduced.

For the purposes of simplification the environment may be classified into four types – clear water, phytoplankton, nitrifying bacteria and heterotrophic bacteria; there may, however, be several types of organism. The limits provided by the biomass or water replacement rate between the two environments are intended to indicate the order of magnitude rather than state absolute values.

It is important to check carefully the reaction of stock to the different environments and to have the means of rapid action, i.e. changing water and oxygenation.

Check carefully reactions of shrimps in the different environments.

Table 17   The different cultural environments

Management will be different in each of the following four cases.	
Shrimps	Environmental characteristics
Low density	Environment 1 Transparency of over 1 m Little chlorophyll – clear water pH of 8.5
Growth	Environment 2 Slight transparency Much chlorophyll – green water pH of 8.5 Fluctuating oxygen content
High density	Environment 3 Very limited transparency Variable chlorophyll content pH over 8 Low oxygen content during the day Large amount of nitrogen (ammonia, nitrites, nitrates)
High density	Environment 4 Very limited transparency pH of 8.5 Stable oxygen content during the day Absence of nitrogen salts

Overall management of a commercial shrimp farm

As has already been seen, setting up and running a large project requires several operations in conjunction; its success can only be judged by its development and the harmony of the various operations.

The following plan is suggested for a farm with a production capacity of 500 tonnes per year. The operations may be as follows:

136

- controlled production of juveniles – at the hatchery
- rearing – on the farm
- food production – at the feed mill
- processing – at the processing plant
- marketing – by the sales department.

To organise these five essential operations, secondary liaison operations – transport and communication – are required. A project is said to be integrated when it includes all these operations. In most cases, however, feed is produced by an independent livestock feed mill. Nevertheless, those responsible for large projects often check the quality of ingredients and feeds produced. In addition, the hatchery is often on a different site away from the farm. A typical plan is suggested below.

Management of a project
Since it is economically advantageous to use the same technical services for the hatchery, farm and processing unit – even if these units are all separate – they will be coordinated by a manager. He is generally more directly concerned with running the farm since he is in charge of administration and finance. An experienced biologist, assisted by an assistant biologist, is appointed to be responsible for technical management, especially in the initial stage, and for the transfer of technology.

The technical management staff are responsible for:
- the hatchery
- logistics – in conjunction with the project manager
- the post-larval pre-rearing unit
- the rearing unit
- the processing unit.

The hatchery
Management of the hatchery involves several operations:
- management of the broodstock
- monitoring maturity
- monitoring disease
- production of *Artemia* nauplii
- production of single-cell algae
- rearing larvae.

Rearing broodstock
Broodstock are reared in earthwork ponds according to an established procedure. Work at the hatchery is carried out by a small team supervised by the person responsible for monitoring maturity.

Monitoring maturity
This is important since it affects the production of post-larvae from the hatchery. It must be managed by an experienced biologist, who will supervise:
- broodstock rearing
- the monitoring of maturity
- spawning and hatching.

Monitoring disease
Monitoring the health status of post-larvae on a daily basis is essential if diseases are to be quickly identified and treated. It should be carried out by a trained and experienced biologist.

Production of artemia nauplii
This is also important but does not present any particular technical difficulties. It may be supervised by a competent technician.

Production of single-cell algae
Algae are an essential feed for young shrimp larvae. Algae culture is difficult and the procedures must be followed carefully. A specialist, assisted by a competent operator, should manage the production of algae.

Rearing larvae
This is the principal function of the hatchery. Workers engaged in production of post-larvae must be supervised by a highly qualified biologist with knowledge of shrimp diseases; he will be assisted by at least two operators.

The logistics section
This section has the following responsibilities:
- producing electricity for the whole project
- the functioning of the hatchery (filters, water, air)
- supplying fresh water
- maintaining the processing unit
- supplying sea water
- supplying compressed air to the pre-rearing unit
- maintaining transport equipment (outboard motors, lighters, dinghies)
- motor vehicles
- preparing and using equipment for harvesting shrimps from the rearing ponds and transporting to the processing unit
- general maintenance of buildings and ponds
- monitoring and treatment of effluent waste levels

- protecting the installations.

This section should be managed by an engineer who receives instructions either from the project manager for operations requiring coordination, or directly from the processing unit manager, or the technical manager for work of a specific routine nature on each unit.

The engineer is assisted by technicians and specialists from each of the areas for which he is responsible.

The pre-rearing unit

Pre-rearing often takes place intensively in a nursery. In view of the highly specialised nature of intensive pre-rearing, this unit is often managed separately by a biologist. This unit is used for the pre-rearing of post-larvae which come from the hatchery at sizes P4 to P5 and up to P25.

The rearing unit

Rearing takes place on this unit according to a pond management plan prepared by the technical management department. A highly specialised biologist should be responsible for the rearing unit.

In view of the size of the project, sub-units are often set up, each managed by a specialist. In addition to the general work, they are responsible for the routine work of feeding, checking water quality, sampling and cleaning filters, and monitoring the health of stock.

The staff responsible for these units calculate the weekly feed requirements and ensure that the unit operation plans prepared by the project management are complied with.

Harvesting is also planned by the rearing unit, in conjunction with the technical management staff, which takes its instructions from the general management. The general management will therefore also give instructions to the processing supervisor.

The processing unit

Shrimps are processed as soon as they are harvested. The unit works closely with the rearing units and general management.

The unit is responsible for processing, packing and preserving the shrimps until they are dispatched. At each stage of processing the ambient temperature, which varies from one stage to another, must be carefully controlled.

The principal stages in the processing/preservation chain are:
- the production and storage of ice
- storing harvested shrimps prior to processing
- processing shrimps – washing, peeling, sorting, treating, packing, weighing

- freezing
- storage before dispatch, and putting in containers.

The quality of the product is particularly important. The unit is therefore often managed by a processing specialist, assisted by a refrigeration technician. During the technology transfer stage, biologists may assist the teams of supervisors (biologists, technicians, engineers) from each unit.

15 Processing and marketing

15.1 *Harvesting and packing*

Harvesting

Harvesting shrimps from a pond must be carried out at night and the whole operation needs to be completed at least two hours before sunrise. It is important that this procedure should be followed, to maintain product quality by avoiding the risk of overheating in the pond and while the shrimps are being taken to the processing unit. If it has been necessary to use antibiotics during grow-out, harvesting should only be carried out after the appropriate drug-withdrawal period. With large ponds, in order to stagger processing, partial harvesting of some shrimps will be necessary, before harvesting the remainder.

Partial harvesting
This is carried out using fixed equipment put into position in the ponds over several days, or by seining, or electrically.

Fixed nets generally consist of one or more catching chambers. The mesh used depends on the size of shrimps to be harvested. Shrimps harvested using this type of equipment will not be spoilt if they are removed frequently.

Total harvesting
After several partial harvests, the final harvesting will be done by draining the pond so that the remaining shrimps go into a sump outside the outlet monk. However, for certain species it is sometimes preferable to use electrical methods.

If the bottom of the pond has a steady slope and the water flows easily, the shrimps generally come out without any problem. They can also be removed by using special pumps in the outlet monk.

Processing must be done very soon after harvesting.

Processing

Shrimps are sometimes sold live or fresh. The species *Penaeus japonicus* is sold almost entirely in this way; the market is very specialised but very limited.

Tropical species are sold frozen and generally exported. There are two stages in processing.

Pre-treatment
Six operations are involved.

Sorting
This is carried out by hand on grids to remove waste, i.e. vegetable, fish and mineral debris.

Washing
This is done to remove dirt from the shrimps. After washing the shrimps are put into plastic bags, about 20 kg to a bag.

Weighing
This gives an account for the shrimps harvested.

Treatment with sodium metabisulphite
This is to satisfy the market and importing country regulations. The shrimps are immersed in a two per cent solution of sodium metabisulphite for about three minutes. This anti-oxidant is used to retard the development of melanosis, particularly on the cephalo-thorax.

Draining
The shrimps are allowed to drain for a few minutes.

Packing with ice
The bags are filled with ice flakes and sent either directly for prep-aration for dispatch or to a cold chamber where they are stored at 0°C.

All pre-processing is generally carried out on the farm in an open shed.

Processing
Shrimps are preferably sold on European, North American and Japan-ese markets. They are either processed whole or peeled, depending on market requirements.

The stages in the processing chain are basically as follows.

142

Reception
The shrimps are put in a washing tank to remove the ice.

Peeling
Peeling is done by hand by workers on both sides of a table. The tails are put into a tank of iced water at the end of the table before being taken to a mechanical sorter.

Sorting
After a final inspection, the tails are taken by elevator to the sorter. Since sizes do not vary greatly, sorting into five classes is generally sufficient.

Pre-packing
After leaving the sorter, the tails are put onto tables for drying and putting into special packs to retain their shape. These are then weighed and sent to the freezing room.

Freezing
It is essential that shrimps are frozen to −35°C in a few hours, although the process employed varies.

Final packing
The packs are packed in tens in cartons then put onto pallets in a refrigerated container at a temperature of between −18°C and −22°C.

A standard 20 foot container may hold 9–10 tonnes of shrimps; a 40 foot container will hold 18 tonnes.

15.2 *The prawn and shrimp market*

Tropical marine prawns and shrimps represent approximately 85 per cent of the total world prawn production, which in 1989 was over 2 500 000 tonnes.

It is thought that exploitation of natural stocks has now reached its maximum level. The increase in world production of marine prawns and shrimps is primarily due to the great progress made in aquatic farming. It was estimated that in 1990 the production of farmed prawns and shrimps, amounting to about 600 000 tonnes, could reach 30–35 per cent of world production by 1992 (two per cent of the total 1981 production).

Most countries engaged in prawn or shrimp farming are in Asia or Latin America. They are principally the Republic of China, Taiwan,

Thailand and Indonesia in Asia, and Ecuador, Panama and Columbia in Latin America.

Consumer countries are almost entirely the industrialised countries. Prawns and shrimps are still a luxury product, although their consumption has been encouraged by a tendency for prices to fall appreciably as a result of increased production. In the USA, for example, the growth in their popularity has been very steady and they are now appearing in fastfood outlets.

There are two large classes of sea prawns:
- tropical prawns (principally penaeids)
- temperate prawns (pandalidae and shrimps).

USA, Japan and Western Europe (EEC) consume over 50 per cent of the world production.

The American market

The American market, 30 per cent of which is supplied nationally, is the largest in the world (1.3 kg per inhabitant per year). Demand is mainly for tropical prawn tails. More than 50 per cent are consumed in restaurants.

The USA is the second largest importer by volume (229 000 tonnes in 1988). The apparent consumption of nearly 380 000 tonnes therefore makes it the largest market in the world (16 per cent of the world production).

The Japanese market

The characteristics of the Japanese market are the small proportion produced nationally, the high consumption per inhabitant (2.5 kg per year), very high quality requirement, a demand for high value products (very large prawns and even live prawns sold to the consumer at up to US$120 per kilogram) and finally some diversity in the form of products sold.

With over 260 000 tonnes imported in 1988, or nearly 30 per cent of the tonnage of prawns imported worldwide, Japan is the largest importer of prawns and shrimps in the world.

National production is about 60 000 tonnes per year. Apparent consumption is about 320 000 tonnes, representing 13 per cent of world production.

The European market

The European market varies considerably. Average consumption of prawns and shrimps per inhabitant is about 500 grams per year, varying from 2.3 kilograms in Denmark to 300 grams in West Germany. In contrast to the American and Japanese markets, the proportions of common shrimps and temperate shrimps consumed, which constitute most of the European production, is very high. The consumption of tropical prawns varies quite considerably according to the country. Very little is consumed in the northern EEC countries where the product is virtually unknown, while in the south (Italy and Spain) it is very popular and larger quantities are consumed.

As a group, EEC countries are the third largest consumer of marine prawns in the world (175 000 tonnes in 1985).

Among the principal European markets are France, where apparent consumption in 1985 was about 35 000 tonnes, Great Britain, which consumed about 30 000 tonnes, Italy, which consumed over 28 000 tonnes and Spain, the biggest consumer, 50 000 tonnes.

Most of the very small numbers of prawns from farms in France are sold locally. French prawn imports are very high and represent the largest item of imported marine products.

Up to 1985 it was principally the import of temperate shrimps which was increasing, but in the last three years there has been a considerable increase in the import of tropical prawns. Frozen prawns, which account for about 80 per cent of the market, include:

- temperate shrimps (not including prawns) which are mainly imported from Denmark
- prawns, mainly from Ireland
- common shrimps from the Netherlands
- penaeid shrimps, mainly from African countries (65 per cent), followed by Asia and Latin America.

Marketing is carried out primarily by:

- import companies, which specialise in marine or frozen products
- wholesalers and central purchasing offices which supply most of the French national market (Rungis)
- retailers (restaurants and shops).

Consumers prefer fairly small whole prawns. Large tropical prawns are relatively expensive and still not generally well-known.

One of the characteristics of the French market is that a large proportion of penaeid shrimps is sold ready cooked and frozen (or thawed).

The European market (France and Spain) is at present considered to be developing fast and prices are appreciably higher than on other markets (USA and Japan). It is also a seasonal market, with peak consumption during national holidays. Prices therefore depend on several factors such as seasonal demand fluctuation, the origin and type of prawns and exchange rates.

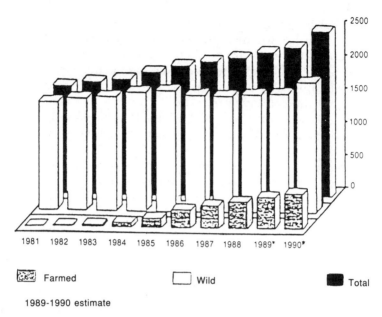

Farmed   Wild   Total

1989-1990 estimate

Fig 68   *World production of shrimps 1981–1990 in thousands of tonnes live weight (source: LMR Shrimp Market Report)*

Prices

Prawns and shrimps are classified according to size, which indicates the number of animals per pound or kilogram.

Over 80 per cent of prawns sold throughout the world are processed, peeled and classified using British standards, i.e. the number of prawn tails per pound.

Table 18   Changes in prices of shrimps from Ecuador on United States wholesale markets between 1982 and 1987 (in US$ per 500g of peeled shrimp)

White shrimps from Ecuador	Class 26–30 (tails 15–18 g)	Class 31–35 (tails 13–14.5 g)	Class 36–40 (tails 11–12.5 g)
1982	6.05	4.95	4.45
1983	5.75	5.35	5.05
1984	5.20	4.65	3.90
1985	4.50	4.00	3.85
1986	6.10	5.35	5.05
1987	5.10	4.15	3.65

146

The price of prawns and shrimps depends on several factors:

- **species**: tiger shrimps are the most expensive, followed by white shrimps
- **size**: price is proportional to size, the bigger the prawn the higher the price
- **source of supply and pack quality**.

Prices take all these factors and seasonal fluctuations into consideration. Like any raw material, prices depend on supply and demand and also on factors which are much less foreseeable, associated with changes in the world economy and exchange rates.

Bibliography

Section 1

Arrignon, J., *L'écrevisse et son élevage*, ed. Bordas, librairie Dunod, 30, rue St-Sulpice, 75006 Paris, 1981

Arrignon, J., *Cria del Cangrejo de rio*, ed. Acribia, Royo 23, 50006 Zaragoza, Spain, 1984

Arrignon, J. and Blin, F., *Effets de l'apparition en Région Parisienne de l'écrevisse rouge des marais de Louisiane*, Aqua Revue 33, October-November 1990, 25-30, 1990

Avault, J.W. Jr. and Huner J.V., 'Crayfish culture in the United States', in Huner, J.V. and Brown, E.E. (ed), *Crustacean and mollusk aquaculture in the United States*, AVI Publishing Company, Westport, Connecticut, USA, 1985, pp. 1–62

Delibes, M., and Adrian, I., 'Effects of crayfish introduction on otter *Lutra lutra* food in the Donana National Park, SW Spain', *Biological Conservation* 1987, 42, pp. 153-159

Feminella, J.W. and Resh, V.H., 'Submersed macrophytes and grazing crayfish: a study of herbivory in a California freshwater marsh', Holarctic Ecology, 1989, 12, pp. 1–8

Gault, J., *Ecrevisses en Louisiane*, Voyage d'études en juillet 1977, published by ADA (Association pour le Développement de l'Aquaculture), 1978, 5, pp. 1–25

Hobbs H.H. Jr., 'Crayfishes (*Astacidae*) of North and Middle America', in *Biota of Freshwater Ecosystem, Identification Manual no. 9*, US Government Printing Office, Washington, DC, USA, 1972

Huner, J.V. and Barr, J.E., *Red swamp crawfish, biology and exploitation*, The Louisiana Sea Grant College Program, Center for Wetland Resources, Louisiana State University, Baton Rouge, Louisiana 70803, USA, 1984

Huner, J.V. and Barr, J.E., *Crawfish in the classroom*, Louisiana Department of Education and Sea Grant College Program. Center for Wetland Resources, Louisiana State University, Baton Rouge, Louisiana 70803, USA, 1984

Jaspers, E. and Avault, J.W. Jr., *Environmental Conditions in Burrows and Ponds of the Red Swamp Crawfish Procambarus clarkii (Girard) near Baton Rouge, Louisiana*, Proc. Ann. Conf. South-Eastern Assoc. Game and Fish. Comm. 23, pp. 634–647

Laurent P.J. and Forest J., 'Données sur les écrevisses qu'on peut rencontrer en France', La pisciculture français, 11, rue Milton, 75009 Paris, 54, 1979

Lowery, R.S. and Mendes, A.J., '*Procambarus clarkii* in Lake Naivasha, Kenya, and its effects on established and potential fisheries', *Aquaculture*, 1977, 11, pp. 111–121

Miltner M. and Avault, J.W. Jr., 'Rice and millet as forages for crawfish', *Louisiana Agriculture*, 1980, 24 (3), pp. 8–10

Pfister V.A. and Romaire, R.P., 'Catch efficiency and retentive ability of commercial crawfish traps', *Aquacultural Engineering*, 1983, 2, p. 101

Section 2

Aquacop 1983, Intensive larval rearing of *Macrobrachium rosenbergii* in recirculating system, first international biennial conference on Warm Water Aquaculture, Crustacea, 9– 11 February 1983, Brigham Young University, Hawaii

Cohen D., Ra'ananz Z. and Brody T., 'Population profile development and morphotypic differentiation in the giant freshwater prawn *Macrobrachium rosenbergii* (de Man)', Journal of World Maricultural Society, 1981, 12 (2), pp. 231–243

Griessinger J.M., 'L'élevage de la chevrette *Macrobrachium rosenbergii* en Guyane: plan de développement, bilan, perspectives', *Aqua Revue*, 1986, 7, pp. 21–24

Griessinger J.M., Robin Th., Pollet Th. and Pierre M.J., 'Progress in use of biological filtration in mass production of *Macrobrachium rosenbergii* post-larvae in closed system in French Guiana', presented at 'Aquaculture 89', 1989, 12–16 February, Los Angeles, CA, USA

Johnson S.K., 'Diseases of Macrobrachium', in M.B. New (ed), *Giant Prawn Farming: Developments in Aquaculture and Fisheries Sciences* 10, Elsevier Publishing Co., Amsterdam, 1982, pp 269–277

Lacroix D. and Falguière J.C., 'Procédure d'ensemencement, de restockage, d'alimentation et de récolte de *Macrobrachium rosenbergii* en système continu', Second version, Rapport CNEXO–FA – Martinique, 1984, p. 23

New M.B. and Singholka S., 'Manual for the culture of *Macrobrachium rosenbergii*', FAO ed. Rome, Fisheries Technical Paper, 1982, 225, p. 116

Nip W.K. and Moy J.H., 'Effect of freezing methods on the quality of the prawn *Macrobrachium rosenbergii*', Proc. World Maricultural Society, 1979, 10, pp. 761–768

Ra'anan Z., 'The ontogeny of social structure in the freshwater prawn *Macrobrachium rosenbergii*', Doctoral dissertation, The Hebrew University, Jerusalem, Israel, 1982, pp. 101

Sandifer P.A., Hopkins J.S. and Smith T.I.J., 'Observations on salinity tolerance and osmo regulation in laboratory reared *Macrobrachium rosenbergii post-larvae (Crustacea: Caridea)*', Aquaculture 6, 1975, pp. 103–114

Shang Y.C., 'Comparison of freshwater prawn farming in Hawaii and Thailand: culture, practices and economics', Journal of World Maricultural Society, 1982, 13, pp. 113–119

Smith T.I.J., Sandifer P.A., Jenkins W.E. and Stokes A.D., 'Effect of population structure and density at stocking on production and commercial feasibility of prawn (*Macrobrachium rosenbergii*) farming in temperate climates', Journal of World Maricultural Society, 1981, 12 (1), pp. 233–250

Section 3

Aquaculture, G. Barnabé, vol. 2, Lavoisier, 1986

ASEAN, Manual on Pond Culture of Penaeid Shrimp, FAO/UNDP, 1978

Hanson and Goodwin, *Shrimp and Prawn Farming in the Western Hemisphere*, Dowden, Hutchinson and Ross Inc. USA, 1977

IFREMER publications:
Fiches biotechniques de la Station d'Aquaculture de Saint-Vincent (Nouvelle Calédonie)
Rapports et Fiches de la Station Aqualive (Noirmoutier)
Rapports et Fiches Merea (Palavas-les-flots)
Rapports et Publications d'Aquacop (Tahiti)

Glossary

Aerobic of conditions for organisms or biological and chemical processes which can only live/take place in the presence of oxygen

Algal bloom proliferation of single-cell algae in the surface layer of stagnant water giving it a characteristic colour

Anaerobic living in an environment without air or oxygen

Anode positive electrode (as opposed to cathode)

Anoxic lacking or deprived of oxygen

Bait an edible substance or attractive object put into the water or into a trap to attract fish or crustaceans

Benthic living on the bottom of a water course or a stretch of water

Biological cycle life cycle of a living being, from birth to death, through the adult reproduction phase (when rearing animals, the biocycle extends from birth to reproduction)

Biomass the amount of living matter in an aquatic ecosystem per unit of volume or surface area expressed in units of mass (living matter derived from benthos, plankton, and even from higher animals)

BOD (Biochemical Oxygen Demand) the amount of oxygen needed to destroy or break down organic materials in water, with the aid of micro-organisms which develop in the environment under certain circumstances

Bow the forward part of a boat or ship

Buffer capacity capacity of an inorganic or organic mineral, or by extension the environment containing it, to stop changes in pH by fixing or releasing H^+ ions

Carbohydrates organic compounds consisting only of carbon, hydrogen and oxygen; they are glucides (sugars, starches, etc.)

Cathode negatively-charged cathode (as opposed to anode)

Chitin organic substance similar in structure to cellulose {polyholoside – $(C_6H_9O_4)_{10} (OH)_2 (NH_2)_8 8 H_2O$}, which makes up the **cuticle** of crustaceans and insects

Chitinolytic bacteria bacteria which attack **chitin**

Citric acid triacid alcohol which may be extracted from lemon juice

Cohort group of individuals having lived through the same event during the same period of time

Common name name of an animal or plant in common language; the scientific name is given in Latin

Cuticle external membrane of certain animals (such as crustaceans), containing *chitin*

Decomposer, decomposing agent living organism making up the benthic micro-fauna which takes part in the break down of organic matter into minerals, e.g. small crustaceans, insect larvae, worms, protozoa and bacteria

Dietary relating to the balance of nutrients

Dredge or trawl track see *seine*

Dystrophic of an environment with excess organic material which results in lack of oxygen and the ultimate disappearance of most living organisms

Ectocommensal an organism living on the outer surface of a different species to the benefit of one without harming the other

Endocommensal an organism living inside another organism to the benefit of one without harming the other

Endogenous produced on the site

Enzyme a protein substance which facilitates and increases a biochemical reaction. There are many specific enzymes which play an important part in the physiological processes of all living organisms (the names of enzymes terminate in -ase, e.g. diastase, zymase)

Epizootic diseases epidemic diseases affecting animals

Euryhaline living equally comfortably in either salt or fresh water

Eutrophic rich in nutrients, having abundant plant growth and hence little oxygen

Eutrophication phenomenon relating to water with abundant nutrients and phytoplankton which may result in a reduction of oxygen content

Exogenous introduced from outside

Exoskeleton external skeleton, shell, carapace

Exotoxin bacterial toxin released in the surrounding medium, spreading into the environment

Fish fry the young of fish, morphologically different from adults

Formalin common name for formaldehyde (CH_2O) used for washing and disinfecting instruments or premises, treating diseases, pickling or preserving anatomical parts and animals

Formol see *Formalin*

Fry see *Fish fry*

Genotype the genetic constitution of an individual resulting from genes inherited from the parents (as against *phenotype*)

Gradient rate of variation of a physical magnitude, i.e. pressure, temperature, in relation to distance

Heterotrophic relating to organisms which require external organic substances for nutrition

Inboard a marine engine mounted inside a small boat (opposite of outboard)

Integument husk, rind, shell or other natural covering

Interface surface forming a common boundary separating two parts, materials or pieces of equipment, e.g. soil/water, seawater/freshwater

Intertidal relating to the coastal area between high and low tide

Isothermal relating to the same temperature

Larva embryonic form with an independent life but unlike the final form of the animal, e.g. nauplius in crustaceans

Lentic relating to still or stagnant water or water with a very slight current

Life cycle biological cycle of a living organism from birth to death, from the adult reproduction stage (in cultures from birth to the reproductive period)

Lipid a fatty substance containing a fatty acid, e.g. oil, fat, lard, butter

Lotic relating to swiftly flowing, turbulent water

Malachite green pure oxalate of malachite used to disinfect the eggs of fish or of crustaceans

Mineralisation changing an organic element into a mineral element by the action of micro-organisms

Non-baited device uses no bait to attract fish or crustaceans (traps with baits are active)

Oviduct the duct or tube through which the ovum (ovule, oocyte) passes on leaving the ovary

Ovigerous carrying or producing eggs or ova

Paludal relating to marshes

Passive not attracting fish or crustaceans by bait (a baited trap is active)

Periphytic characterising all organisms living on surfaces but attached to a base, formed mainly of higher aquatic plants

Petasma male sexual organ of the sea prawn

Phenotype individual properties of an organism taken as a whole, corresponding to the formation of a *genotype,* as determined by the interaction of environmental factors during the development of the organism

Phyletic or phylogenetic relating to the evolutionary inter-relations of the forms found in the ascendants of a species (relating to Phylum which means 'trunk')

Planktonic relating to all the minute organisms living and floating in water, passively or otherwise, but incapable of effectively resisting or moving against currents. Phytoplankton is the vegetable constituent of plankton; zooplankton is the animal constituent of plankton

Pleuron, pl. pleura extension of the carapace forming a semi-rigid membrane

ppm parts per million (one milligram per kilogram = one ppm)

Productivity organic production capacity of an environment or specific stock

Proteolytic relating to the breakdown of proteins during metabolic processes (enzymes, for example)

Protide general term for nitrogenous substances containing amino acids such as peptides and proteins

Quarantine isolation (initially 40 days) imposed by public health regulations on living creatures which may be carrying infectious diseases

Rotenone a product of certain plants (Derris) used to kill fish, which may then be eaten

Secchi disc 20 cm diameter disc with four equal sectors painted black and white used to measure water opacity

Seine triangular net for fishing, pulled along smooth bottoms in shallow water

Sessile not having a peduncle, e.g. sessile eye, an eye close to the body

Sex ratio proportion of females to males in a population of a given species expressed as the result of dividing the numbers, or as a percentage

Spermoduct, spermduct duct or tube conveying sperm outside the individual

Stimulus, pl. stimuli external or internal agent that triggers off a nervous system

Systematics science of classification of living forms (by taxonomy or determinant keys)

Thermal gradient rate of variation of temperature

Thelycum female sex organ of the sea prawn

Tidal range difference in height between high and low tides

Trammel, trammel net fishing net consisting of three superimposed nets, the middle one with finer mesh than the other two, and catching the fish in a sort of bag

Trawl action of a trawl or seine net (generally expressed in length of time)

Trawling fishing using a trawl or seine net

Trawl net net comprising a recovery bag and two wings with two

154

cables linking the net to the boat which tows and then lifts it to collect the catch; the net consists of three layers, the middle of a finer mesh than the outer two; fish are caught in the recovery bag

Trophic   relating to nutrition

Uropod   sixth pair of abdominal appendages with the telson, the end part, forming a type of caudal fin in crayfish.

Vernacular name   the common name of an animal or plant in a particular language or dialect, as opposed to the scientific name in Latin

Yearling   fish one year old

Index

Page numbers in *italics* refer to illustrations or tables where these are separated from their textual references.

156